Amphigouri
a comedy of errors for laughter

Paul Diggens has had extensive experience in many of life's roles - as a pirate radio operator, a clerk in the Telephone Manager's Office, a journalist and press officer with the Post Office and for many years Head of PR & Media. Over a period of 20 years or so Paul collected a vast library of so-called circulars and officialdom poking fun at society. These form the basis of *Amphigouri* with the added mix of new material in creating a book of laughs !

Amphigouri
a Comedy of Errors for Laughter

Paul Diggens

Arena Books

First published in 2020 by Arena Books

Arena Books
6 Southgate Green
Bury St. Edmunds
IP33 2BL

www.arenabooks.co.uk

Distributed in America by Ingram International, One Ingram Blvd., P.O. Box 3006, La
Vergne, TN 37086-1985, USA.

Paul Diggens
Amphigouri a comedy of errors for laughter

British Library cataloguing in Publication Data. A Catalogue record
for this book is available from the British Library.

ISBN-13   978-1-911593-67-6

BIC classifications:- FA, FYB.

Cover design
By Jason Anscomb

Typeset in
Times New Roman

Foreword

Trivia in large companies or government departments is normal. It is a way that executives relieve themselves during times of stress or decision making, to fulfil their day by creating funnies or passing them down the line to impress their staff.

Government departments, one-time nationalised industries – there's no exception. Unlawful use of the photocopier is commonplace.

This collection is over a period of more than 20 years, working as a civil servant, a Post Office Telephones clerk, and in The Post Office. Many thanks to all who have contributed to my funny file, including my dear colleague the late Mick Heath, and the many contacts throughout the public relations industry who have given to the files.

The first selection here were the original Funny File entries way back in the days of Post Office Telephones, and their internal courses: Language and the Public. These are genuine extracts from letters sent to the Pensions Office, Insurance Companies, the Gas Board, plus language and the public at the Post Office.

We continue through the Funny File with a mixture of 'linked' subjects. Special thanks to star proofreader, Sharon Whitehead, without whose help this would never have been published!

Paul Diggens (MIPR)

CONTENTS

-1-
Unfortunate Errors

PENSION OFFICE

1. I cannot get sick pay. I have six children. Can you tell me why this is?

2. This is my eighth child. What are you going to do about it?

3. Mrs R. has no clothes and has not had any for a year. The clergy have been visiting her.

4. In reply to your letter, I have already co-habited with your office, so far without result.

5. I am forwarding my marriage certificate, and two children, one of which is a mistake as you can see.

6. Sir, I am glad to say that my husband, reported missing, is now dead.

7. Unless I get my husband's money, I shall be forced to lead an immortal life.

8. I am writing these lines for Mrs G. who cannot herself write. She expects to be confined next week and can do without it.

9. I am sending you my marriage certificate and six children. I had seven and one died, which was baptized on a half sheet of paper by the Rev Thomas.

10. Please find out if my husband is dead, as the man I am now living with won't eat or do anything until he is sure.

11. In answer to your letter, I have given birth to a little boy weighing

ten pounds. Is this satisfactory?

12. You have changed my little girl into a little boy. Will this make any difference?

13. Please send money at once as I have fallen into errors with my landlord.

14. I have no children as my husband is a bus driver and works all day and night.

15. In accordance with your instructions, I have given birth to twins in the enclosed envelope.

16. I want money as quick as you can send it. I have been in bed with my doctor all week and he does not seem to be doing me any good.

17. Milk is wanted for my baby as the father is unable to supply it.

18. Re your enquiry. The teeth in the top are all right, but the ones in my bottom are hurting horribly.

INSURANCE

1. The accident was due to the other man narrowly missing me.

2. Lorry halted and worked for the Corporation.

3. I collided with a stationary tramcar coming in the opposite direction.

4. The occupants were stalking dear on the hillside.

5. I left my Austin 7 outside, but when I came out later, to my amazement there was an Austin 12.

6. To avoid collision I ran into the other car.

7. There were plenty of lookers-on but no witnesses.

8. The water in my radiator accidentally froze at 12 midnight.

9. Car had to turn sharper than was necessary owing to an invisible lorry.

10. I was scraping my nearside on the bank when the accident happened.

11. After the accident a working gentleman offered to witness in my favour.

12. I collided with a stationary tree.

13. There was no damage done to the car as the gatepost will testify.

14. Accident was due to the road bending.

15. The witness gave his occupation as a gentleman, but it would be more correct to call him a garage proprietor.

16. The other man altered his mind and I had to run into him.

17. Ice on the road applied brakes causing skid.

18. I told the idiot what he was and went on.

19. One wheel went into the ditch. My foot jumped from brake to accelerator pedal, leapt across the road to the other side and jumped into the trunk of a tree.

20. I remember nothing after passing the Crown Hotel until I came to and saw PC Brown.

21. A bull was standing near and a fly must have tickled him because he gored my car.

22. A cow wandered into my car, I was afterwards informed that the cow was half-witted.

23. She suddenly saw me, lost her head, and we met.

24. I was taking a friend home and keeping two yards from each lamp post which were in a straight line. Unfortunately, there was a bend in the road bringing the right-hand lamp post in line with the other and of course I landed in a ditch.

25. If the other driver had stopped a few yards behind himself, it would not have happened.

26. I bumped into a shop window and sustained injuries to my wife.

27. I bumped into the lamp post which was obscured by human beings.

28. I heard a horn blow and was struck violently in the back. Evidently a lady was trying to pass me.

29. I misjudged a lady crossing the street.

30. Coming home I drove into the wrong house and collided with a tree I haven't got.

31. Three women were all talking to each other, and when she stepped back and one stepped forward I had to have an accident.

32. I can't give details of the accident as I was somewhat concussed at the time.

33. Wilful damage to the upholstery was done by rats.

34. A pedestrian hit and went underneath my car.

35. I blew my horn but it would not work as it was stolen.

36. A lamp post bumped into my car, damaging it in two places.

37. My car was stolen and I set up a human cry but it has not been recovered.

38. The car in front stopped suddenly and I crashed gently into his luggage grid.

39. I left my car unattended for a minute and whether by accident or design it ran away.

40. The other car collided with me without giving warning of his intentions.

41. I unfortunately ran over a pedestrian and the old gentleman was taken to hospital, much regretting the circumstances.

42. On entering Wales I blew my horn at the left-hand corner.

43. I thought the side window was down but it was up as I found out when I put my head through it.

44. I considered neither vehicle was to blame, but if either was to blame it was the other one.

45. I was proceeding along the road at moderate speed when another car rushed out of a side turning and turned upside down in a ditch. It was his fault as he said.

46. I knocked over a man – he admitted it was his fault, as he had been knocked down before.

47. I looked for the sign but the more I looked the more I couldn't find it.

GAS BOARD

1. Your fitter wanted us to try it in the fireplace but we think it is better in the cupboard.

2. Can you move the meter so that it will not cause an obstruction in my passage.

3. The electric man did it through the floorboards but your man put it in my front passage where everyone can see it.

4. Since you put a new pipe from the mains into our house my husband and I dread going to bed because of a slight discharge. We think there is a leak just before it enters.

5. We have heard there are two ways you can have it, and it works out cheaper the more you get if you have it the other way.

6. I am not satisfied with an apprentice so will you send me a man to do it properly.

7. My wife will be ready for your man if you will let me know when he is coming on a postcard.

8. We will try to pay before the month ends as my husband will be surprised if you cut it off without telling him.

9. My husband is pretty handy but he says your men can do it better because of their tools.

10. It has gone slack with use and my husband cannot make it tight no matter how he tries, so for the time being we are making do with an

old rag.

11. My slot is not blocked now, but your men made an awful mess banging their tools on the wall.

12. Since I made an arrangement with your salesman I am having a baby and would like to change it for a drying cabinet.

13. My neighbour has a bigger one than me and it makes a difference to her water when she is filling the bath.

14. My husband is under the impression that I am getting it at reduced rates but your salesman did not use his head and got me into trouble.

15. It is about time your workman came to fill the hole because we are fed up with having it in the street. It is a big attraction and we get children by the dozen.

16. A woman who is after this house says she is not keen on it, so if she gets it can your man stand by to take it out before she comes.

17. I have six children. If you do not do something about the leak the coroner will blame you.

18. I told my husband it was safe to leave it in all night but he will not. If he comes to the showroom like I did can the lady satisfy him behind the counter and talk him into it.

19. Will I still need to salt my potatoes after we convert to North Sea Gas?

LANGUAGE AND THE PUBLIC AT THE POST OFFICE

1. I am a German – how do I get married in England?

2. How much is the rail fare to Scotland for an old age pensioner?

3. Could you translate this Friend into English please?

4. I am sorry I have printed my signature but the pen went wrong.

5. What newspapers do you sell?

6. May I have a PROVINCIAL driving licence form please?

7. Can you see if my watch is fully wound?

8. A PRELIMINARY driving licence form, please?

9. Can I have a form for installing a fire alarm?

10. Can you tell me how to spell boutique?

11. Counter Clerk: I'm sorry, you can only renew this motor vehicle licence at a Post Office in the Greater London area.
Customer: Oh, have you got one around here?

12. Three air mail letters, please. They are alright to send abroad, aren't they?

13. If I want to dial 100, do I have to dial 10 ten times?

14. Half a pound of postage stamps please.

15. May I look at the ELECTRICAL roll?

16. Can I have an interfered with form?

17. Counter Clerk: Can I have your bank book please?
Customer: No sorry I've burned it.

18. Has anyone handed in a skirt? I lost it in the telephone kiosk yesterday whilst making a call?

19. Can you tell me if a telephone call was made from Colchester to Australia yesterday? I don't know the number that was called.

20. Can you mend my umbrella please?

21. I've come to join your tv club.

22. Customer to Counter Clerk: How do I spell my name please?

23. Counter Clerk: The road vehicle licence forms are under the picture. (Customer proceeds to remove picture from wall.)

24. A dozen and eight stamps please.

25. Is it worth saving these days?

26. You give us pensioners all the dirty notes – they do in London too.

27. Can you tell me what year it is please?

28. Is my husband's cricket bat here – he lost it yesterday?

29. Excuse me, but I've put my iron on my telephone wire and melted it.

30. Have you a Great Yarmouth DICTIONARY please?

31. One Customer to Another: Excuse me, but you are on fire.

32. Woman Customer to Counter Clerk: I have left my husband, please tell me what to say so that he will take me back.

33. One disabled stamp please.

34. Excuse me but do you know there is a woman lying on the floor?

35. I've been riding horses, so I think I ought to be able to learn to drive alright, don't you?

36. Customer: I'm moving house – can you tell me what to do?
Counter Clerk: Take the furniture with you.

37. How do I adjust my barometer for sea level because it's lower where I live?

38. Please don't give me thin £5 notes.

39. My sister has just put 2p up the reject slot of the telephone.

40. Do you sell stamps?

41. Can I have a form for a licence for a 17 year old?

42. Excuse me, a cat has jumped through the slot into the letter-box.

43. No, I'm sorry I have no evidence of identity – only my birth certificate.

44. Can I have 3 badgers and 3 hares please? (British Wildlife Stamps)

45. Can you tell me what I do to get a request played on the radio?

46. Can you go abroad with a passport?

47. I've pushed my front door key into the slot in the station telephone kiosk.

WERE YOU EVER READY FOR THE COMMON MARKET?

1. Trafficators – Die Blinken Lightenmitticken Furturnen

2. Bonnets – Der Fingarpinscher und Kopfchoper

3. Exhaust Pipe – Das Spitzenpoppen Bangentuben

4. Speedometer – Der Egobooster und Lineschootinbackeruppen

5. Air Horne – Der Vhatderhellvosdat Klaxenfanfaren

6. Puncture – Das Pflatt mit Dammundblasten

7. Learner Driver – Dumkopf Elplatt

8. Estate Car – Der Schnogginwagon mit Bagzeroomfurrompinderback

9. Mini – Der Buzzboxen mit Traffiksveerinfistshaken Underfinger Raisen

10. Petrol – Das Koslijooze fur Geddinsegreezeoffendentrousen

11. Motor Club – Der Mettighous fur Wagennatterin Elbowraisen und Chaddenupziebirds

12. Parking Meter – Das Tannerpinscher Blockenverks

13. Windscreen Wipers – Das Flippenfloppen Muckschpredunsticken

14. Cross Roads – Das Kussundschveeringstrassen

15. Roundabout – Das Eeochezitatsisschlost

16. T-Junction – Das Vergutenssake Dontgostraitonnenkorner

17. Power Brakes – Dis Shtoppinverks mit Edbangenon Dervindscreen

In those past dark days of coal and power strikes …

FUEL AND POWER EMERGENCY

How to save fuel in the home:

Britain is facing a serious reduction in its supplies of oil, coal and electricity – a situation which could rapidly get worse.

So, we must all act now and increase our efforts to save fuel. Check the points below and take action immediately.

1. Extinguish all fires, especially those that use gas, coal and electricity.

2. Put on as many clothes as you can. At present there are no restrictions on how many clothes you can wear.

3. Climb into bed. But do NOT use hot water bottles, as an acute water shortage is imminent.

4. Turn out the light. If everyone in the country uses no light or fires at all, supplies of electricity could last indefinitely.

5. Set fire to your house by rubbing two pieces of wood together. One blazing house will provide much needed warmth for hundreds of people in addition to creating vacant sites suitable for office development.

6. Try and die as soon as possible. This can be done by starvation. Your early death will help MPs to win the next election.

CUT FUEL CONSUMPTION NOW.

Issued by the Department of Trade and Industry for HM Government.

AND WITH POLITICS IN MIND …

Our Father which art in Downing Street,
Harold be Thy Name.
United Kingdom gone,
We shall be done on earth, and probably in heaven.
Give us this day our dearer bread
And forgive us our devaluations,
As we forgive them that speculate against us.
Lead us not into the Common Market,
But deliver us to the unions.
For this is the Kingdom, no power, no Tory,
For ever and ever. Amin.

THE 1990 151ST PSALM

Thatcher is my shepherd,
I shall not want,
She leadeth me beside still factories,
She guideth me to the path of unemployment for her party's sake.

I fear no evil for thou art against me,
She annointest my wages with price increases,
So that my expenses runneth over my income,
Surely poverty and hard living shall follow me,
And I shall dwell in a mortgaged house for ever.

Five thousand years ago, Moses said:
"Pack your camel, pick up your shovel, and mount your ass,
And I will take you to the promised land."
Five thousand years later, Roosevelt said:

"Lay down your shovel, sit on your ass and smoke your camel,
for this is the promised land."

Today, Thatcher will take your shovel, sell your camel,
Kick your ass and tell you there is no Promised Land.
I am glad I am British, I am glad that I am free,
But I wish I were a DOG and Thatcher a TREE.

DAYS IN THE CIVIL SERVICE ALWAYS BEGIN AND END
WITH THE SHORT FORM OF SERVICE FOR GOVERNMENT
OFFICIALS:

PRAYER
Grant that this day we come to no decision
Neither run into any kind of responsibility
But, that all our doings may be ordered
To establish new departments.

HYMN
Thou who seest all things below
Grant that Thy servants may go slow,
That we may study to comply
With regulations till we die.
Teach us, O Chief, to reverence
Committees more than common sense,
Impress our minds to make us plan
To pass the baby when we can.

And when the Tempter seeks to give
Us feelings of initiative,
Or when, alone, we go too far
Chastise us with a circular.
Mid war and tumult, fire and storms
Strengthen us we pray, with forms.
Then will Thy servants ever be
A flock of perfect sheep to Thee.

BENEDICTION
The peace of Whitehall
Which passeth all understanding,
Preserve your mind in lethargy,
Your body in inertia
And your soul in coma.
Now and forever,
Amen.

And with the Government there are circulars … and then there are 'Circulars'!

An extract from a Government Circular giving guidance on the application of the Sex Discrimination Act:

"The Act makes provision for sex to be regarded as a genuine occupational qualification in certain circumstances. Details are at Appendix A. Alas no diagrams."

THE DEPARTMENT OF LICENSING AND REGISTRATION

COMPACT DISC PLAYER LICENCE REMINDER

It has recently been brought to our attention that you are in possession of a Compact Disc Player. From our records it seems you are unaware that an owner's licence is required for possession of this property, as these devices are included under the Legal Firearms Statutes (revised 1985).

The Compact Disc Player, in its domestic form, is equipped with a high intensity laser which is regarded as a firearm for the purposes of the above legislation. Whilst it is perfectly safe in everyday use, it may be illegally converted into an offensive weapon. For example, lasers in the more expensive CD players have an effective range of 750 metres, whereas the lasers in cheaper models, whilst only having an effective range of 200–250 metres, are no less deadly in their potential.

To retain possession of the player you must, in the next seven days, apply at the Post Office for a Compact Disc Player Licence (ask for form PH3755) and register the equipment at your local police station. Your local authorities will then take steps to satisfy themselves of the precautions you are taking against theft, such as secure housing (a wall safe for example) and perimeter deterrents like a house alarm system. Furthermore, you will be required to undertake to the same authorities your willingness to surrender said property in times constituted as a national emergency. Your co-operation is appreciated.

For the Department of Licensing and Registration.

-2-
Civil Defence & Trouble in the Office

And it seems Government Departments issue special circulars:

NUCLEAR CIVIL DEFENCE

In the event of a Nuclear Attack Alarm:

1. Open all windows and doors.

2. Descend from all upper floors to ground floor.

3. If possible, descend to basement levels.

4. Where available, use underground shelters previously fitted out with emergency food, water, first aid, oxygen and anti-radiation supplies.

5. If caught outside or on upper levels, remove all loose articles, i.e. spectacles, rings, necklaces, watches, neckties, earrings, etc.

6. Slacken all tight clothing and loosen buttons.

UPON SEEING FLASH, BEND DOWN, PUT YOUR HEAD BETWEEN YOUR KNEES AND KISS YOUR ARSE GOODBYE.

And the following letter was produced in case it happens …

CIVIL DEFENCE PROGRAMME

Dear Sir,

Under the direction of the Civil Defence Authority we are entering into extensive training to organise both civilian and industrial corps for the purpose of fire-fighting in the event of the danger of 3(cj9/7) atomic raids becoming imminent.

As a citizen whose loyalty to the Government is unquestionable, we believe that we can count on you as a patriot for full co-operation.

We have, therefore, taken the liberty of appointing you Atomic Fire Warden for your local area. Training will be confined to one night per week for the next six months. You will be advised on the training venue shortly.

Please accept the thanks of the Committee for your co-operation in this enterprise, which we feel is so vital to the best interest of us all.

Yours sincerely,
R.U. Awake

List of Equipment for ATOMIC RAID WARDEN:

Respirator.
Axe to be carried from belt.
Stirrup pump to be carried over left shoulder.
Extending ladder to be carried over right shoulder.
Long household shovel to be carried under left arm.
Rake to be carried under right arm.
Scoop to be carried under right arm.
Whistle to be carried in mouth.
Belt to be worn around waist with ten hooks for carrying 4 sandbags and 6 pails of water.
Two wet blankets to be slung around neck.
Flashlight to be carried on back.
Tin helmet to be worn with brim upturned for carrying extra water (for drinking only).
Box of matches to light atomic bombs that fail to ignite.
Extra sand (fine) to be carried in all pockets.

Ship's anchor to be dropped in case warden breaks into fast gallop. Broom (stiff or birch) to be inserted in any available place, so that warden may sweep floor as he progresses.

Upon completion of training, the above equipment will be delivered to you and should be kept where it can be found quickly. We suggest near the front door of your residence, to facilitate speed in getting to the devastated areas requiring your help.

MEMORANDUM: To All Members of Staff

From: Company Safety Officer

Date: 31st February 1987

Re: Media Coverage of Aids

Following recent Government Guidelines the management feel it prudent to advise their official standing on this matter.

1. It will now be your responsibility to ensure that all staff in your section DO NOT SHARE NEEDLES.

2. All internal mail can only be 'licked' by Registered Blood Donors who have not changed partners for the last four years. This is obviously designed to reduce the risk of spreading the virus throughout the company.

3. Any person sharing a cup or a telephone will have to wear a condom.

4. All toilet seats are to be burnt after use.

5. Any person caught sitting in another person's chair not wearing a condom will be severely reprimanded.

6. Should any member of staff require medical attention, it is imperative that the person administering the treatment uses a condom.

7. All ignorant persons are to be encouraged to seek employment elsewhere.

8. In the unlikely event of any person dying on the premises, you should arrange for a fork-lift truck to remove the corpse to the Account's Department, where it is expected that the incident will not be noticed until pay day.

TO ALL STAFF:

Re: EXCESSIVE ABSENCE

Due to the excessive number of absences during the past year, it has become necessary to put the following new rules and procedures into operation immediately.

1. SICKNESS. No excuse. The Management will no longer accept your Doctor's Certificate as proof. We believe that if you are able to go to your Doctor, you are able to attend for work.

2. DEATH (your own). This will be accepted as an excuse. We should like two weeks' notice however, since we feel it is your duty to train someone else for your job.

3. DEATH (other than your own). This is no excuse. There is nothing you can do for them, henceforth no time will be allowed off for funerals. However, in case this should cause some hardship to some of our employees, there are those who might care to note that on your behalf the Management has a special scheme in conjunction with the local council for lunchtime burials, thus ensuring that no time is lost from work.

4. LEAVE OF ABSENCE FOR AN OPERATION. We wish to discourage any thoughts you may have of needing an operation and, henceforth, no leave of absence will be granted for hospital visits. The Management believes that as long as you are an employee here, you will need all of whatever you already have and should not consider any of it being removed. We engage you for a particular job with all your parts and having anything removed would mean that we would be getting less than we bargained for.

5. VISITS TO THE TOILET. Far too much time is spent on this particular practice. In future, the procedure will be that all personnel shall go in ALPHABETICAL ORDER. For example: those with surnames starting with A will go from 9.00–9.45am, B will go from 9.45–10.00am, etc.

Note: Those of you who are unable to attend at your appropriate time will have to wait until the next day, when your turn comes again.

8 RULES FOR A SHORT LIFE –
REGULATIONS FOR EXECUTIVES WHO DON'T ENJOY LIFE:

1. Always put your work first and yourself second.

2. Do everything possible to go to your office, even after dinner in the evenings, on Saturday afternoons and on holidays.

3. If you can't stay late in the office, take a full briefcase with you to work on at home.

4. Don't try to relax during meals – even better, turn each break into a discussion if you can.

5. Don't allow yourself any pleasure. It is all a waste of time and gets in the way of concentration.

6. The same could be said for holidays. It's better to give them up.

7. Never say no to an invitation: accept especially invitations to conferences, meetings, and assemblies.

8. Never shirk one atom of your responsibilities and take everything on your own shoulders – in fact you are indispensable.

If you follow these rules, your firm had better look around for someone who should soon take your place.

BUT for the minor grades …

The Union is my shepherd,
I shall not work.
It maketh me lie down on the job.
It leadeth me beside the still factories.
It restoreth my insurance benefit,
Yes, though I walk through the shadow of decreased productivity
I will feel no recriminations, for the union is with me.
Its restrictive practices, and shop stewards comfort me.
It prepareth a works committee for me in the presence of my
employers.
It anointeth my hands with pay rises, my bank balance runneth over.
Surely hire purchase payments and union dues shall follow me all the
days of my life.
And I shall dwell in a council house for ever.

THE BOSS

The Boss is right.
The Boss is always right.
Should a subordinate be right, Article 1 will apply.
The Boss doesn't eat, he sustains himself.
The Boss doesn't drink, he tastes.

The Boss doesn't sleep, he rests.
The Boss is never late, he is delayed.
The Boss never leaves his job, he is called out.
The Boss entertains no relationship with his secretary, he is educating her.
The Boss never reads the newspapers during working hours, he studies them.
One enters the Boss's office with one's own ideas; one leaves with the Boss's.
The Boss remains the Boss, even in swimming trunks.
The more one criticizes the Boss, the lesser the bonus.
The Boss has to think for everyone.

CONCLUSIONS

The Boss is a Dictator – one must prevent Bosses from marrying to avoid an increase in their numbers. Whenever a subordinate's ideas are good – they are no longer his, but the Boss's.

TAKING TIME OFF

What the Boss says about a day off ...

So, you want a day off.
Let's take a look at what you are asking for.
There are 365 days per year available for work.
There are 52 weeks per year in which you already have two days off per week, leaving 261 days available for work.
Since you spend 16 hours each day away from work you have used up 170 days, leaving only 91 days available.
You spend 30 minutes each day on a coffee break.
That accounts for 23 days per year, leaving only 68 days available.
With a one-hour lunch period each day you have used up another 46 days, leaving only 22 days available for work.
You normally spend 2 days a year on sick leave.
This leaves you only 20 days available for work.

We are off for 5 holidays per year, so your available working time is down to 15 days.
We generously give you 14 days' vacation per year, which leaves only one day available for work …
And I'll be damned if you're going to take that day off.

ALWAYS REMEMBER – The Boss has a title. Use it – 'Wotsisname' won't do. More suitable epithets will gain four pints of real ale at the next drinks party.

BENEATH THE BOSS ARE MANAGERS AND SUPERVISORS …

When the body was first made, all parts wanted to be Supervisors.

The brain insisted, "Since I control everything and do all the thinking, I should be Supervisor."

The feet said, "Since we carry man where he wants to go we should be the Supervisors."

The hands said, "Since we do all the work and earn all the money to keep the rest of you going, we should be the Supervisors."

The eyes too staked their claim, "Since we must watch out for all of you, we should be Supervisors."

And so it went on – the heart, the ears and, finally, the bum. How all the other parts laughed to think the bum should be the Supervisor.

Thus, the bum became mad and refused to function. The brain became feverish, the eyes crossed and ached, the legs got wobbly, and the stomach went sick.

All pleaded with the brain to relent and let the bum be Supervisor. And so it came to be that all the other parts did their work, and the bum simply supervised and passed a load of crap.

MORAL – YOU I HAVE TO BE A BRAIN TO BE A SUPERVISOR.

WHEN IT COMES TO A COCK-UP, NOBODY DID IT …

This is the story about four people named Everybody,
Somebody, Anybody and Nobody. There was an important job to be done and Everybody was sure that Somebody would do it. Anybody could have done it, but Nobody did it. Somebody got angry about that because it was Everybody's job. Everybody thought Anybody could do it, but Nobody realised that Everybody wouldn't do it. In the end Everybody blamed Somebody when Nobody did what Anybody could have done.

AND THIS IS THE STORY OF WHY I FIRED MY SECRETARY

Two weeks ago, it was my fortieth birthday, and I wasn't feeling too hot that morning anyway. I went into breakfast knowing that my wife would be pleasant, say 'Happy Birthday' and probably have a present for me. She didn't even say 'Good Morning', let alone 'Happy Birthday'.

Well, that's wives for you. But the children came into breakfast and didn't say a word either. When I started off to the office, I was feeling pretty low and despondent.

As I walked into my office, Millie, my Personal Assistant did say 'Good Morning Boss and Happy Birthday', so I felt a little better as someone had remembered.

I worked until noon. At noon Millie knocked at my door and said, "As it's such a lovely day, and it's your birthday, how about going out for lunch, just the two of us?"

I thought it was a great idea, so we went to lunch. We didn't go where we normally go; we went into the country to a little private place. We had two drinks each and enjoyed lunch tremendously. On the way back to the office she said that as it was a beautiful day, we didn't need to go back to the office, but we could go back to her apartment for more birthday drinks.

So, we went to Millie's apartment. We enjoyed more drinks and smoked a cigarette. She then said, 'Boss, if you don't mind, I think I'll go into the bedroom and slip into something more comfortable – and I allowed her, as I didn't mind at all. She went into the bedroom and about six minutes later she came out carrying a big birthday cake, followed by my wife and children. All were singing Happy Birthday … and I sat there with nothing on but my socks.

BUT ...

We the most willing, led on by the unknowing,
Are just doing the impossible, for all the ungrateful.
We have done so much, with only a little,
For so damned long, we are now fully qualified,
To do almost anything with ABSOLUTELY NOTHING!

WHICH REMINDS ME OF A FRIEND'S BIRTHDAY –
or – ONCE UPON A TIME … BOOM!

Richard had a maddening passion for baked beans. He loved them, but they always had an embarrassing and somewhat odorous reaction on him. However, one day he met a girl and fell in love. When it became apparent that they would marry he thought to himself, "She's a sweet gentle girl. She'll never go for this kind of carrying on, so I must make the supreme sacrifice and give up beans." They married.

Some months later his car broke down on the way home from work and, since they lived in the country, he would have to walk home. He phoned his wife and told her he would be late. On the way home, he passed a small eating house and the smell of freshly baked beans was overwhelming.

Since he still had some miles to walk, he figured he could work off any ill effects before he got home … and so he stopped for a meal. Before he came out he had eaten three large orders of baked beans. All the way home, he phut-phutted merrily and so felt reasonably safe when he got to his front door. His wife was excited at his arrival and said, "Darling, I have the most wonderful surprise for dinner tonight as it's your birthday." He had quite forgotten that it was his birthday.

She then blindfolded him and led him to his chair at the head of the table. He seated himself and, just as she was ready to remove the blindfold, the phone rang. She made him promise not to remove the blindfold until she returned, then she went to answer the phone.

He seized the opportunity, shifted his weight to one leg and let fire. It was not only loud, but ripe. He shook his napkin and vigorously fanned the air about him.

He just had things back to normal when he felt another explosion coming. With amazing rapidity, he then shifted his weight to his other leg and let go again. This one was a true prize-winner. He again had to clear the air as well as he could.

Keeping his ear to the conversation in the hall, he went on like this for some minutes until he heard farewells coming from the direction of the phone and knew that his wife would return. He arranged his plate, silverware and napkin as well as he could in front of him. Smiling silently, he awaited her return. After apologizing for taking too long she asked if he had peeped and he, of course, answered quite truthfully, that he had not.

With a flourish she removed the blindfold and there, to his surprise, were …

Twelve dinner guests seated around his table!

WHICH BRINGS US TO THE GRAND FARTING COMPETITION
…
(passed under the International Rules of Farting)

To Be Held at The East German Farting Stadium

Fart Off: 8.40pm   Final Fart: 12 midnight

Referees:
  1.Former Farting Champion (all Classes) of Egypt, Lebanon
(National Services).

  2. Wet Fart Champion of the United Kingdom and Isle of Man.

Chairman: Who still holds the World Record Duration Fart for 9
seconds (unbeaten after training on, Duck Eggs, Barm Cakes and
Mushy Peas).

Rules:
When called, each competitor will step on the raised platform and
must lower his trousers on the platform and not before.

He will grip the farting post: any grip will be permitted, one hand or
both.

At a given signal from the senior referee, the competitor will
commence to fart.

A SHIT IS IMMEDIATELY DISQUALIFIED.

Grading: Dry farts, long farts, wet farts, short farts, alternating long-
and-short farts, rip-raps, bubbles, blobs and squeaks.

The Judge will take into consideration the quality of all farts – strength, odour, posture of competitor and grip used. Cushion dusters, blanket rippers, and thunderclaps are admissible. Echo Chambers will NOT be allowed.

After the final fart a demonstration will be given by the World Champion Farter. Also, by a runner-up who came within 1 second of the World Champion, but was disqualified for shitting. The Thunder Box Farting Formation Team will give a display of Formation Farting.

The audience are requested not to fart during the competition as this upsets the judge.

The drinking of alcohol and the eating of peanuts is not permitted during the contest as this causes the arse to quiver, which distorts the farts, and gives a false sound.

NOW WHAT ABOUT THE 'F' WORD?

Perhaps one of the most interesting words in the English Language is the word – F**K. It is one magical word. Just by its sound you can describe pain, displeasure, ill-feeling and hate!

In language, 'F**K' falls into many grammatical categories:
It can be used as a verb both intransitive (Dave f****d Ann), and the transitive (Ann was f****d by Dave).

And also as an adverb (Ann is a good f**k).
Perhaps as an adjective (Ann is f*****g beautiful).

As you can see, there are not many words with the versatility of f**k.

Besides the sexual meaning of the word, there are also the following:

GOODBYE   F**K OFF.

GREETINGS   HOW THE F**K ARE YOU?

FRAUD	I GOT F****D AT THE CAR AUCTION.
DISMAY	OH F**K IT!
TROUBLE	WELL, I GUESS I'M A F****D MAN.
AGGRESSION	F**K YOU.
DIFFICULTY	I UNDERSTAND THE F*****G JOB.
DISPLEASURE	WHAT THE F**K IS GOING ON HERE?
INCOMPETENCE	HE F***S UP EVERYTHING.
LOST	WHERE THE F**K ARE WE?
RETALIATION	GET OFF YOUR F*****G ARSE!

And remember General Custer's last words …
"Where did all those f*****g Indians come from?"

Also, the last words of the Mayor of Hiroshima …
"What the f**k was that?"

And last, but by no means least, those immortal words of the Captain of the Titanic …
"Where is all that f*****g water coming from?"

STANDARD OF DRESS – HOT WEATHER

The current hot spell is making conditions somewhat uncomfortable, but I am sure you will realise that a reasonable standard of dress must still be maintained.

As a number of visitors regularly call at this office, it is essential that the right impression is given.

If you have any doubts about what is regarded as reasonable, you should consult your own Supervisor for advice – but I have listed a few instances that will NOT be accepted:

The wearing of shorts, non-wearing of shoes, over-colourful or designer shirts, T-shirts for men.

I am sure you will agree that the last item should be included to keep up standards. However, I would expect ladies to continue with their usual sense and taste if wearing a garment that could otherwise be described as a T-shirt.

THE UNIFORM AND CLOTHING BRANCH.

-3-
Time Scales & Vacancies Applied For

APPOINTMENT TIMESCALES

We also find appointments at work are important in timescales …

Friendly call	10 minutes
Salesmen with good deals	Half second
Life Insurance Agents	15 seconds
Wine Salesmen with free samples	2 hours
Friends inviting us to lunch	2 hours
Friends wishing to talk soccer and golf	Most of the day
Those wishing to pay bills	All day
Customers	8 hours
Wives	No time
Girlfriends	All night
Wealthy relatives in their 80's	Any time
Relatives wanting jobs	3 seconds

NOW TO SICK LEAVE …

HEREWITH A SELF-CERTIFICATION OF A NOTIFIABLE
ILLNESS FORM:

This form must be submitted at least 21 days before the date on which
you wish illness to commence.

Name:

Department: Works Number:

Date on which you wish illness to commence:

Nature of illness you wish to suffer from:
(Applications to suffer from pregnancy must be accompanied by
No 36/54/9E consent of husband/boyfriend)

Have you ever applied to suffer from this illness before?
If so, give date.

Do you wish illness to be slight/severe/crippling/fatal?

If fatal, do you wish this to be considered a permanent disability?
(Applicants wishing to suffer fatal illness should indicate on the foot
of this form whether they wish the company to be represented at the
funeral/cremation)

Do you wish to suffer at: Home / Hospital / Costa Brava / Anfield?

Do you wish the illness to be of a contagious nature?

If so, indicate approximate number of people you wish to infect.

Have you ever been refused permission to suffer from an illness?
If so, give details.

Do you wish your wife/husband to be informed of your illness, if he/she contacts the firm regarding your whereabouts?

I, the undersigned, declare that to the best of my knowledge the answers given above are the truth and accurate.

Signed: Date:

Applicants are reminded that all applications will be considered on merit and that more than three applications per annum will be considered excessive and not in the best interests of the company. Under no circumstances will any employee be permitted to suffer more than one fatal illness: any person disregarding this warning, render themselves liable to dismissal.

AND THIS IS A DO-IT-YOURSELF SICKNESS BENEFIT CLAIM FORM:

(Dissatisfied by the Government's new self-certification arrangements for the sick, a new form has been designed.)

Name of Employee: Name of Employer:

Address: Address:

1. Give date on which you deemed yourself to be unfit for work.

2. State briefly why you deem yourself to be unfit (first read notes below).

Do not say poorly, groggy, under the weather, indisposed, knackered, a touch of mange.

Do not use over-colourful descriptions, e.g. Montezuma's Revenge, Inca Quickstep, Delhi Belly, Turkey Trots, Churchyard Cough, Black Death.

Do not list advertisers' diseases, e.g. sinking feeling, ashtray breath, dishpan hands, the greasies.

Avoid use of martyr, as in 'martyr to rheumatism'.

If you suffer from an anti-social complaint avoid invidious references to other nations, e.g. The French Disease, The Italian Disease, but Maltese Fever and Hapsburg Lip are acceptable.

   3.   How sick are you?
If you are not as sick as a parrot, what are you as sick as?

   4. Did you have to be revived by the kiss of life before you were able to collect this form? Yes or No.

   5. Do you regard your own conduct as in any way contributable to your condition – (think carefully).
Were you engaged in a domestic brawl, a pie-eating contest, resisting a mugger, jogging, glue sniffing, a rugby celebration?

   6. In addition to your illness entered in (2), do you suffer from any of the following?
Delayed shell-shock (do not list battles before 1914).
Agoraphobia (see Note 1).
Asthenia (see Note 2).
Worry about the bomb (see Note 3).
Advanced torpor (see Note 4).

Note 1. Could you advance into the middle of a 50-acre field to collect £100, if it was waiting for you? If you could, you could suffer from agoraphobia.
Note 2. There is no such thing as asthenia.

Note 3. The bomb is not a legitimate reason for absence from work, unless it is actually dropped.

Note 4. If when you are lying on your back, a brimful tumbler of water placed on your chest does not overflow, you need not complete the form, as you will no longer require State Aid.

7. During your self-certificated absence from your job, have you:
Operated your car as a minicab?
Given video exhibitions to a male audience for gain?
Gone shopping with your family to Boulogne?
Taken a holiday of more than three days overseas?

8. Have you ever certified yourself as ill before or after:
A Bank Holiday?
A Christmas Fortnight?
A Cup Final?
A Test Match?
A Papal Visit?
A Royal Wedding?

9. Give the date on which you propose to return to work, if you can see no other course.

10. Would you be willing to have your condition investigated by a panel of six faceless medical experts, answerable only to the State? Yes or No.

DECLARATION – I understand that any false information in the foregoing may bring past my head the Utmost Rigour of the Law.

I claim whatever benefit is going.*

I wish to forget the whole thing.*

(*Strike out whichever line is inapplicable.)

Signature of applicant: ....

THEN THERE ARE THE PROBLEM LETTERS RECEIVED IN
GOVERNMENT DEPARTMENTS ...

Dear Sir,

Can you please advise me on the following problem?

I am 28 years of age and have two brothers and two sisters.

Being a working-class family, we all support the Labour Party – with
the exception of one of my brothers, who is a Conservative. He is a
Lavatory Attendant at the Home Office and regards himself as a Civil
Servant, which makes him feel superior. This naturally causes a lot of
discord in the family.

My other brother is serving a seven year sentence at Dartmoor for
repeated rape and arson. My two sisters are on the streets and father is
living on their earnings. Mother (that's what I usually call her) is
pregnant by the next door neighbour and father, glad of the excuse,
now refuses to marry her.

Recently I met a charming girl who is an ex-prostitute, single, and the
mother of three fine children. I think a great deal of her and my
problem is I am closer to and love dearly my brother. I think I have
mixed genes, and obvious homosexual tendencies.

Should I tell her about my brother being a Conservative?

Yours sincerely.

SIMILARLY, A LETTER TO A MAGAZINE PROBLEM PAGE ...

Dear Problem Page,

I am a man aged 24 and come from a large family.

My name may be familiar to you as my youngest brother plays for West Ham football club. My other brother is unfortunately serving life in Broadmoor for multiple rape and driving while disqualified. My two sisters had their own business called 'The Erotics Visiting Massage Service', but gave it up when they realized they had lesbian tendencies towards each other.

My mother is mentally retarded and an alcoholic and refuses to have anything to do with my father since she discovered he is a practicing homosexual who recently contracted aids. She is now pregnant by the Pakistani who runs the Off-Licence and Doctors say her heroin addiction may affect my unborn half-brother.

Whilst inside I have been writing to a charming girl of my own age, an ex-prostitute with six lovely children. We plan to marry when I get out and her syphilis clears up.

My problem is, how can I tell her about my brother playing for West Ham?

Yours sincerely.

FORMS FOR JOB APPLICATIONS CAN BE FRIGHTENING …

Address: (please give town, street, house room, bed and shift number)
West Indians may give minibus or car number: ……………..
Degree of suntan:
(light / medium / dark / very dark / matches Ace of Spades)
Are you visible after sunset? Yes or No.

Car (West Indians only)
Please give the following details about your car:
What type of Ford Cortina is it?
Amount of Fur Trim?
Number of Spotlights?

Percentage of rear screen obstructed by dangling ornaments/stickers?
Percentage of front screen obscured, as above?
Total power in megawatts of rear lighting?
When did you last consider insuring your car?
When was it last taxed?
When did it last fail the MOT?
How did you acquire your car?
(state theft / HP fraud / scrapyard / MOT failure / any other method)

PARENTS
Name of Mother? .... Name of Father? (if known)
....
(West Indians should list all possibilities on a separate sheet)

Father's Occupation: bus conductor / lavatory attendant / pusher /
steel band / drummer / underground guard / Her Majesty's artist
(delete as appropriate)

Marital Status: single / shacked-up / common-law marriage /
informal liaison

Number of children: Illegitimate ….. / Legitimate ….. (if any)

Hobbies: (tick as appropriate)
Mugging   Prostitution   Dope Pushing   Dominoes   Other

Asians only – when did you illegally enter Britain?

Income: (list your current income from these sources)
Proceeds from: Theft ………. Prostitution ……….
Social Security ……….. Fraud ………. Slums ………. High Rents
……….

Diet: (please tick your staple diet)
Curry   Rice   Pet Food   Potatoes

Asians only:
Are you toilet trained? Yes or No.
(What is toilet training?)

Please return the completed form together with a recent photograph.
West Indians and Asians may omit the photograph as you all look the
same.

BUT IN DAYS OF OLDE …

Dear King Arthur,

I wish to apply for a job as one of your knights. I have long admired
your ruling of the country and I would like to enter your employment.
Seeing that Percival and Gawain are not having any luck in finding the
Holy Grail, I could prove invaluable.

Along with my ability to find Grails, I am also skilled in sword fighting,
jousting and strategically retreating. When you and your brave
followers are away fighting, I could remain at Camelot to defend it. I
could also look after Excalibur and polish it, so that it is ready for you
to use in battle.

My past experience includes rescuing several maidens in distress by
single-handedly removing spiders from their baths and I once freed a
princess who was chained to a stake, awaiting the dragon. The dragon
was very grateful as her screams were giving him a headache.

As I was top of the form in chemistry, I may be able to give Merlin
some useful hints and help him keep a firm hand on Morgana who is
giving you a spot of trouble at the moment.

If Lancelot and Guinevere are planning to spend their holidays on the
Lake again this summer, I could arrange their bookings as I have had
previous experience in a travel agency organising pilgrimages to the
Holy Land.

If there should be no vacancies in your party of knights, I wish to be considered as a spare round table as I have sturdy legs and a good hard top.

Yours sincerely,
Peabody (Sir)

AND …

In days of olde, when knights were bold
And toilets weren't invented,
They dug a hole in the middle of the road
And sat there, quite contented!

A DREAM OF PARADISE

I come to England poor and broke,
Go on the dole, see labour bloke.
Fill in form, have lots of chatters
Kind man give me lots of akkers.*   *(money)

I thank him much and then he say
"Come next week and get more pay."
You come here we make you wealthy,
Doctor too, to make you healthy

Six months on dole, got plenty money,
Good Pal meat to fill my tummy.
Send for friends from Pakistan,
Tell them to come as quick as can.

Plenty of us on the dole
Lovely shirt, and big bank roll.
National Assistance is a boon,

All the dark men in it soon.

They come here in rags and tatters,
Go down dole and get some akkers.
They come with more, we live together
One bad thing – the bloody weather!

One day white man come inside,
Ask me if we wash in Tide.
I say yes, me wash in Tide,
Too damn cold to wash outside!

All get nicely settled down,
Fine big house in busy town.
Fourteen families living up,
Fourteen families living down.

All are paying nice big rent,
More in garden live in tent.
Soon I send for wife and kids,
They not have to live in digs.

Still vote labour, draw more dole,
Good old Neil, bless his soul.
Wife wants glasses, teeth and pills,
All are free, we get no bills.

White man good he pays all year,
To keep the National Assistance here.
Bless all white men, big and small,
For paying tax to keep us all.

We think England damn good place,
Too damn good for white-man race.
If he not like the coloured man –
Plenty room in Pakistan!

HOW ABOUT WORKING AS A CHRISTMAS CASUAL?

Good King Wenceslas looked out
On the feast of Stephen,
Invoices lay round about
Deep and Crisp and even.
Brightly shone his crown that night
With one un-mortgaged jewel,
When the postman came in sight
Dwarfed by burden cruel.

"Hither page come stand by me,
Look there through the curtain.
Is there ought that we can do
To lighten his cruel burden?"

"Indeed Sire," said the hard-worked page,
"Join him as a part-timer.
Then Christmas with your Royal wage
Might be somewhat finer."

So, the good king got the hint
And started a new fashion.
And, overjoyed, the Royal Mint
Took turkey off the ration.

The fashion's still alive today
– Christmas Casual Labour –
And sending off this form's the way
To earn cash and help your neighbour.

(I am over 16!)

HOW ABOUT THIS VACANCY AD IN A POST OFFICE
PUBLICATION?

Designer for PO Official Calendar DPOOC 1990 (one post)

Applications are invited from suitably qualified staff for the
temporary post of Designer for the PO Official Calendar (1990).
(DPOOC (1990). This post is open to both men and women, although
candidates who are totally sexless may be considered to have special
qualifications. The successful candidate will be answerable to the
Director in Charge of Censorship of Naughty PO Calendars
(DICOCONPOC). The post will initially have the same grading as the
successful candidate, but a really successful candidate can expect
immediate promotion to Chief Tea Trolley Pusher at POHQ
(CTTPAPOHQ).

Duties:
DPOOC (1990) will be expected to produce a 365-sheet calendar for
the year 1990 (February 29 will be deemed not to exist to keep down
the PO wage bill). Each sheet will contain a suitable illustration
showing the delights of working for the Post Office and a motto of
exhortation to the staff, e.g. "WORK IS FUN, WORKING HARDER
IS EVEN FUNNIER" is thought to be acceptable, but "ON THE 31st
MAY, YOU GET YOUR PAY" is definitely not. DPOOC 1990 will
also be expected to select appropriately careworn, downcast,
browbeaten, and above all suitably dressed staff over the age of 95 to
act as models. DPOOC 1990 will not accept volunteers other than
postmen willing to be savaged to death by a wolf pack for the theme,
"THE POST NEARLY ALWAYS GETS THROUGH". Such
volunteers will be accompanied in triplicate by a certificate of
insanity issued by Psychological Services Division.

Qualifications:
Applicants are expected to be expert in all the latest paper-rolling
techniques and the technical intricacies of the Kodak Brownie. (The
Society of Post Office Executives are claiming that a PhD in nuclear
physics should be the minimum qualification.)

Membership of the National Viewers and Listeners Association and/or the Festival of Light is essential, although membership of the National Association for Freedom and the UK All Temperance Alliance may be considered exceptionally well-qualified. Fluency in jargon and an ability to invent banal mottoes are essential. Candidates will also be expected to display an aptitude for grovelling to DICOCONPOC.

Conditions:
Detached duty terms will apply except where the successful candidate fails, permanent board and lodging will be arranged at a suitable HM Prison.

Selection:
Short-listed applicants will be invited to attend a selection board consisting of DICOCONPOC, Mary Whitehouse, The Suffragan, Archbishop of Wagga Wagga, the editor of the *News of the World*, the man on the Clapham Omnibus, the Commander of the Metropolitan Police Squad, and Batman.

Applications:
On form PTE 1234567890xyz (TEMP)(DEC'L) should be forwarded together with 33 copies of the current Annual Report to the HofD, Personnel Advice Research Appointment and Selection of Loonies (PARASOL), Room 2, 1st Floor, POHQ Building, by 1st January 1991.

WITH THE POST OFFICE IN MIND …

P120W is an Application Form for Transfer.

A Postman working in Dover, Kent requests, in writing, a transfer to Canterbury, Kent. The desiring reason for transfer – "Able to have children at new accommodation obtained, unable to at present address."

AND A NOTE TO THE POSTMASTER IN 1967 …

Sir,

I am sorry I haven't been able to renew my TV Licence.
I have been under the Doctor and accept full responsibility.

Yours faithfully.

AND NOW IN THE POST OFFICE (or ROYAL MAIL as it's now called) ODE TO TECHNOLOGY …

The changes in the Postage Rates
Don't come in ones, they come in spates,
Machines from which the stamps we vend
Cannot themselves the Tariffs bend,
So, when the charges are increased
The logic of machines is ceased.

Our engineers do try and rush
To modify before we blush,
But 'ere this tricky work is done
It's negative – there's another one.
This problem then does overwhelm
'Cos stamps don't fit the Coin of Realm.

AFTERTHOUGHT …

Or will you settle for 50p
And have your TV Licence free?
Or put machines back on the shelf
And have the Post on the National 'elf?

Pardon me for being cynical

(Rather that than be too clinical)
But LE's arithmetic tricks
May not apply in '86
Unless the total British Nation
Kills this awful thing 'inflation'.

AND HOW ABOUT THE EARLY RETIREMENT PROGRAMME?

As a result of automation and a declining work load, Management must, of necessity, take steps to reduce the current work force. Therefore a Reduction of Employees programme has been devised which seems the most equitable in the circumstances.

Under the plan, older employees will be placed in early retirement, thus permitting the retention of employees who represent the future of the business.

Therefore, a programme to phase out the older personnel (over 40) by the end of the current financial year will be put into effect immediately. This programme will be known as RAPE – Retirement, Aged Personnel Early.

Employees who are RAPED will be given the opportunity to seek other jobs within the business, provided that within seven days of being RAPED they request a review of their employment status.

This phase of the programme will be known as SCREW – Survey of Capabilities of Retired Early Workers.

All employees who have been RAPED and SCREWED may apply for a final review.

This phase will be known as STUFFED – Study of Termination of Use For Further Education and Development.

Programme policy dictates that employees may be RAPED once,

SCREWED twice, but can get STUFFED as many times as Management see fit.

Director Personnel.

ODE TO A WORKER …

If you work and do your best,
You'll get the sack like the rest.
But if you laze and bugger about,
You'll live to see the job right out.
The work is hard the pay is small,
So, take your time and sod 'em all.
'Cause when you're dead, you'll be forgot,
So don't try and do the bloody lot.
Or, on your tombstone, neatly lacquered,
These three words … JUST BLEEDING KNACKERED!

THE PROBLEMS OF DIVIDING GAUL INTO THREE PARTS …

We trained hard … but it seemed that every time we were beginning to form into teams, we would be re-organised. I was to learn later in life that we tend to meet any situation by reorganising – and a wonderful method it can be for creating an illusion of progress while producing confusion, inefficiency and demoralisation.

-4-
No-One Likes Change

IN BRITAIN, NO-ONE LIKES CHANGE …

Here are the BRITISH STANDARD OBJECTIONS:

1. Our work is different.
2. It won't work for a large job.
3. It won't work for a small job.
4. We've been doing it this way for 25 years.
5. We've never done it before.
6. We've tried it before.
7. Another firm tried it once.
8. Why change it? It's working alright.
9. The management will never accept it.
10. The operative, union, builder, architect, consulting engineer, client, etc will never accept it.
11. The .... department says it can't be done.
12. The .... department won't like this.
13. You'll get trouble.
14. It's too radical a change.
15. We're not ready for it.
16. We haven't the time.
17. It's contrary to policy.
18. It will increase overheads.
19. We can't take the chance.
20. We'd lose money on it.
21. It would take too long to pay off.
22. We must appoint a committee to consider it.
23. It's impossible.
24. It needs further investigation.
25. It's too theoretical.
26. It's not my responsibility.
27. We haven't the staff.

28. We haven't the money.
29. I don't like it.
30. Yes … but we must let things do as they are for this year.

You're right, but … NOW DO IT!

VISITORS TO BUSINESSES SHOULD TAKE NOTE OF NOTICES …

e.g. TO THE VISITOR:

Cigarette smoke is the residue of your pleasure. It permeates the air and putrefies my hair and clothes, not to mention my lungs. This takes place without my consent. I have a pleasure also – I like beer now and again. The residue from my pleasure is urine. Would you be annoyed if I stood on a chair and wee'd on your head and clothes without your consent?

SIMILARLY, A STRICT NOTICE IN THE CAR PARK OF A MULTI-NATIONAL …

Date and Time of Parking Offence: ………………..…

This is not a ticket, but if it were within my power to give you one, I would probably give you two. Thanks to your bull-headed and inconsiderate attempt at parking, you have taken room for 3 Corporation buses, 2 elephants, and most of Manchester United Supporters Club. The reason for giving you this, is that in future you may think of someone else other than yourself. Besides I do not like domineering, egotistical or pig-headed drivers and you probably fit into one of these categories, if not all of them.

I sign off wishing you an early transmission failure and the sincere wish that the next time you have the misfortune to be suffering from chronic diarrhoea, you happen to be in the middle of Woolworth's with all the toilets out of order.

With my compliments.

ANOTHER STRONGER ADDITION …

Thanks for parking so close. Next time leave a F****** can opener so I can get my car out. Assholes like you should take the BUS.

SO TO THE LAW AS IT SHOULD BE …

One evening after attending the theatre, two gentlemen were just leaving when they observed a well-dressed, attractive young lady walking ahead of them. One of the men turned to the other and remarked, "I'd give £50 to spend the night with that girl." The lady in question overheard the remark and, to their great surprise, she turned and said, "I'll take you up on that."

Bidding his companion a goodnight, the gentleman thus addressed accompanied the young lady to her flat where they immediately retired to bed for the night.

The following morning he handed her £25 and prepared to leave. She demanded the rest of the money stating, "If you do not give me the other £25, I will sue you." He merely laughed and replied when leaving, "I'd like to see you getting it on these grounds."

The following day he was amazed to receive a summons ordering his presence in court as defendant in a lawsuit. He immediately saw his lawyer and explained the details of the case. The lawyer told him, "She cannot possibly get a judgement against you on these grounds, but it will be interesting to see how her case is presented."

Eventually in court and following the usual preliminaries, the lady's lawyer addressed the court as follows, "Your Honour, my client, this lady here, is the owner of a piece of property, to wit, a garden spot surrounded by a profuse growth of shrubbery. She agreed to rent it to the defendant for a specific length of time for the sum of £50. The defendant duly took possession of the property, used it extensively for the purpose for which it was rented but, upon evacuating the property, he paid the owner £25, one half of the amount originally agreed upon. The rent was not excessive, as it related to restricted property and we ask judgment be granted in favour of the pursuer for payment of the balance."

The defendant's lawyer was both amused and impressed at the way in which his learned friend had presented the case and, to meet it, he made a last minute alteration to the defence he had originally planned. He rose and said, "Your Honour, my client agreed that the lady in question has a very fine piece of property, that he did rent the said property for a time, and great pleasure was derived from the transaction.

"However, that being admitted, I must point out that my client found a well on the property around which he placed his own stones, sunk a shaft and erected a pump, and all the labouring was done by himself. We claim that these improvements to the property were sufficient to offset the unpaid amount and that the plaintiff was adequately compensated for rental of the said property. We ask, therefore, that no judgement be granted."

At this point, the young lady's lawyer jumped to his feet: "Your Honour," he stated, "my client agreed that the defendant did find a well on the property and that he made improvements as stated by my learned friend, but it is our contention that had the defendant not known that the well existed, he would never had rented the property. Furthermore, Your Honour, I would point out that upon evacuating the property, the defendant removed the stones, pulled out the shaft, taking the pump with it, and in doing so, he not only dragged his equipment through the shrubbery, but he left a hole much larger than it was prior to his occupancy, making it easily accessible to little children. We therefore ask that judgement be granted in favour of the plaintiff."

And the lady got it.

DOES DRINKING TAKE PLACE AT WORK AND AT HOME?

Christine Jones, eating peaches and cream,
Saw a ballet performance on her tv screen.
The kids, at the party, watched the movements with awe,
And Chris thought, "I'll show them!" and cleared off the floor.

She started to glide and the kids sat entranced,
Enjoying the scene as she twisted and pranced.
Then she leaped to the ceiling like Anna Pavlova,
But the 'crack' when she landed, meant the dancing was over.

They picked up the pieces, called in the MD,
Who examined her legs (how I wished it was me!)
His final diagnosis, and this news we all know,
Was she'd sprained or she'd cracked a small bone in her toe.

As strange as it sounds, what I've told you is true,
The same thing could happen to me and to you.
We like and respect her, we know she'll be missed …
There's no truth in the tale she was drunk, Brahms and Liszt.

WHO SAID I WAS DRUNK?

I had eighteen bottles of whisky in the cellar, and my wife ordered me to throw the contents of the lot down the sink or there would be trouble. I said that I would fulfil this unnatural request. I withdrew the cork from the first bottle and poured the contents down the sink, with the exception of one glass which I drank. I extracted the cork from the second bottle and repeated the process, again with the exception of one glass which I drank. I then withdrew the cork from the third bottle and poured the whisk done the sink which I drank. I pulled the cork from the fourth bottle down the sink and then poured the bottle down the glass which I drank. I pulled the bottle from the cork of the next and drank one sink out of it, and threw the rest down the glass. I pulled the sink out of the glass and poured the cork down the bottle. I then sink with the glass, bottled the drink and drank the pour. When I had everything emptied, I steadied the house with one hand, counted the glasses, corks, bottles, and sinks with the other, which were 29 and as the house came by I counted them again, and finally had all the houses in one bottle which I drank. I'm not under the affluence of inchol, as some tinkle peep I am. I'm not half as thunk as you might drink. I fool so feelish. I don't who know is me, and the drunker I stand here the longer I get.

Now where's that drinkle of bot gone?

SOME MIGHT HAVE THOUGHT THEY HAD HAD TOO MUCH WHEN THIS WAS BROADCAST …

1st April. TV AM. From today, licences will be required for bicycles and these can be obtained from main Post Offices.

Several people in Kent went into a Post Office to obtain a licence. The Post Office confirmed it was an April HOAX.

GOVERNMENT AND NATIONALISED INDUSTRY OFFICIALS ARE REPORTED ON ANNUALLY.

THE PRACTICE IS CALLED THE ANNUAL APPRAISEMENT – HEREWITH A DEFINITION OF TERMS …

Satisfactory Progress – I can't think of a single interesting thing to say about him.
Easy Going – Bone idle.
Making Good Progress – If you think his work is bad now, you should have seen it a year ago.
Sensitive Person – Never stops whining.
Helpful – Creep.
Reliable – Grasses on his mates.

Adventurous – Will break his neck before the year is out.

Expresses Himself Confidently – Cheeky.

Imaginative – Can always think of something new to put on his self-certificate of sickness absence form.

Easily Distracted – Hasn't produced a single piece of work since his last appraisement.

Works Better in a Small Group – Daren't take my eyes off him for a second.

Needs Praise and Encouragement – Thick as two short planks.

Not Yet Ready for Promotion – He's the only one who knows what this group is about.

Expresses Himself Clearly – Foul-mouthed.

Keen to Do Well – Egotistical.

Work is of a High Standard – His wife wants promotion for him.

Is Easily Upset – Spoilt rotten.

Better at Practical Work – Totally illiterate.

Good With His Hands – Light fingered.

Independent – Obstinate.

Determined – Completely unscrupulous.

Inclined to Daydream – Totally bored with his job.

Good Sense of Humour – Tells endless unfunny jokes.

A Good Speaker – In love with his own voice.

A Quiet Person – Lacking any individuality whatsoever.

Easily Influenced – The group fall guy.

Has a Vivid Imagination – Never short of an excuse.

An Inquisitive Mind – Can't mind his own business.

Often Needs Guidance – Never out of the Guv'nors office.

Good Union Member – Left wing activist.

Good With Figures – Provides an original expense claim.

A Good Judge of Character – Appreciates his Guv'nor is a terrific manager.

AND TO BE A GOOD MANAGER YOU NEED INTELLIGENCE …

Do not start this test until you are told to do so. You will be allowed 10 minutes to complete the test. Mark your answers beside each numbered question. Work as quickly as you can.

1. I went to bed at 8 o'clock in the evening and set the alarm to get up at 9 o'clock in the morning. How many hours sleep would this allow me?

2. Do they have a 4th of July in England?

3. Some months have 30 days, some have 31 … how many months have 28 days?

4. If you had only one match and entered a dark room where there was an oil heater and some kindling wood, which would you light first?

5. If a doctor gave you 3 pills and told you to take one every half an hour, how long would they last?

6. A man builds a house with 4 sides to it, a rectangular structure, each having a southern exposure. A big bear comes wandering by. What colour is the bear?

7. A farmer has 17 sheep. All but 9 died. How many did he have left?

8. Divide 30 by 0.5, add 10. What is the answer?

9. Take 2 apples from 3 apples. What do you have?

10. How many animals of each species did Moses take aboard the ark?

11. If you drove a bus with 42 people on it from Chicago and stopped

at Cleveland to pick up 7 more, and drop off 5 passengers, and at Pittsburgh you drop off 8 and pick up 4, and arrive in Philadelphia 20 hours later, what is the driver's name?

CLEVER, AYE!

These could be the answers ....

1. 1 hour – an alarm can't be set for more than 12 hours unless its electric.
2. Yes.
3. 12.
4. The match.
5. One hour.
6. White – the house must be at the South Pole – thus a polar bear.
7. 9.
8. 70.
9. 2 apples – the question didn't ask how many were left.
10. None – Noah built the ark.
11. If I was driving, the answer is Paul Diggens!

TRY THIS ONE BEFORE WE MOVE TO THE QUESTIONABLE TESTS …

A test of convergent thinking – not more than 15 minutes should be spent on the questions.

1. On average, how many birthdays does a man have in his lifetime?

2. A woman gives a beggar some money. The woman is the beggar's sister but the beggar is not the woman's brother. What relation is the beggar to the woman?

3. A ladder with rungs one foot apart is fixed to the side of a ship. If the bottom rung is just touching the water and the tide is rising at 2 feet an hour, how long will it take for 3 rungs to be submerged?

4. How far can a man run into a wood?

5. Is it ethical in Gretna Green for a man to marry his widow's sister?

6. If 215 football teams enter a knockout cup competition – how many games have to be played to find the winner? (Assuming there are no replays)

7. If it takes 3 cats 3 minutes to eat 3 mice, how long will it take 300 cats to eat 300 mice?

8. If an empty barrel weighs 98 lbs, what do you have to fill it with for it to weight 54 lbs?

9. An archaeologist claims to have found a coin dated 50BC. Do you believe him?

10. A pond doubles in size every year and, after 30 years, it was 100 feet in diameter. In what year was the diameter 50 feet?

11. If a Canadian aircraft carrying American passengers crashes exactly on the border of the USA and Canada, where would the survivors be buried?

12. (optional) Who built the Pyramids?

AND NOW WE GIVE YOU THE ANSWERS …

1. One – the day he was born.
2. Her sister.
3. Never – the ship will rise with the tide.
4. Half way – after that he will be running out.
5. No – if the man has a widow, he is dead.
6. 214.
7. 3 minutes.

8. Holes.

9. No – Christ's birth was not known until it occurred.

10. 29th year.

11. It is not customary to bury survivors.

12. Wimpeys, McAlpines or the Pharaohs (from an Irish GCE paper).

-5-
To the Emerald Isle

SO, TO THE EMERALD ISLE AND A TYPICAL GCE PAPER …

1. Who won the Second World War?

2. Who came second?

3. What is a silver dollar made of?

4. Explain Einstein's theory of Hydrodynamics or write your own name in block capitals?

5. Spell the following: (a) Cat, (b) Dog, (c) Carrot.

6. What is the time of News at Ten?

7. Approximately how many commandments was Moses given?

8. There have been 6 Kings of England called George – name the other 5?

9. Write down the numbers from one to ten.
(Marks will be deducted for every one out of sequence)

10. Who invented Stephenson's rocket?

11. What instrument does Phil the Fluter play?

12. Do you understand Newton's Law of Gravity?
(Answer Yes or No)

13. Of what country is Dublin the capital?
(Candidates must not write on more than two sides of the

paper)

14. Spot the deliberate mistake: An apple a day gathers no moss.

15. Name the odd man out:
Shamus O'Toole, Mahatma Gandhi, Sean O'Flattery, Patrick Murphy.

16. Who is the odd man out:
Cardinal Heenan, The Pope, Jack the Ripper, Archbishop of Canterbury?

17. Is a ducker:
(a) a person who dips biscuits in his tea?
(b) a contraceptive?
(c) a lorry for motorway construction?
(This question need not be answered by Roman Catholics)

18. Name the winning jockey of 1989 Greyhound Derby?

19. In the 1990 Irish Sheepdog trials, how many dogs were found guilty?

20. Who built the Pyramids – McAlpine, Wimpeys, Pharaohs, Thyssens?

Anyone found copying will be awarded double marks for initiative.

ADVANCED LEVEL PAPER FROM THE EMERALD ISLE …

1. What language is spoken by Frenchmen?

2. Give the important characteristics of the Ancient Babylon Empire with particular reference to architecture OR give the first names of the Beatles?

3. What religion is the Pope?

(a) Jewish   (b) Hindu   (c) Anglican
(d) CATHOLIC
(underline one only)

4. What would you ask William Shakespeare to do?
(a) Build a house   (b) Lead an army   (c) Sail the ocean
(d) WRITE A PLAY
(underline one only)

5. What time is it when the big hand is on twelve and the little hand is on ONE?

6. SPELL – London, Dublin, Belfast, Guinness?

7. What country is the Queen of England, Queen of?

8. Where does rain come from?
(a) Supermarkets   (b) USA   (c) A big fountain
(d) THE SKY
(underline one only)

9. Who invented Stephenson's Rocket?
(a) Bobby Moore   (b) Sir Winston Churchill   (c) Dana
(d) STEPHENSON
(underline one only)

10. What is a coat hanger used for?

11. Who is buried in Grant's tomb?

12. How many floors has a two-storey house?

13. How long is the seven-mile Devon tunnel?

14. What is the fastest game in the world?
(a) Ludo   (b) Snap   (c) Chess
(d) PASS THE PARCEL IN A BELFAST PUB

(underline one only)

15. What is the name of the present Prime Minister in England?
(a) Ian Paisley   (b) Malcolm Muggeridge   (c) David Frost
(d) JOHN MAJOR?
(underline one only)

16. What does wood come from?
(a) Cement   (b) Whiskey   (c) The sea
(d) TREES
(underline one only)

17. How many fingers should you have on one hand, excluding the thumb?

18. How many questions (to the nearest three) are there on this paper?

NOW A SEQUENCE WITH APOLOGIES TO THE EMERALD ISLE ...

Heard about the Irishman who is suing Mothers Pride Bakery for using his signature on their buns on Good Friday?

Heard about the Irishman who killed himself jumping off a multi-storey block of flats, because his foreman told him that he had flown in Wellington's during the war?

Why are there only twenty hours in an Irish Day?
Because an Irishman only has ten fingers and ten toes.

How do you tell an Irish Father Christmas?
He has a sackful of Easter Eggs.

Why are there Camels in Egypt and Paddy's in Ireland?
The Arabs had first choice.

Why are there Potatoes in Ireland and Oil in Egypt?
Paddy had first choice.

How can you tell an Irishman in Holland?
He wears wooden wellies.

Four Irishmen sitting in a ring smoking – the police later stated that they had smashed up a dope ring.

Air Lingus pilot, when asked his position, replied: "I'm five feet four inches tall and I am in the front seat."

Paddy fell 3,000 feet down a wall. Murphy shouted, "Have you broken anything?" Paddy replied, "There is nothing to break down here."

Captain of an Air Lingus jet is identified by the Three Gold rings on his wellies.

How do you brainwash an Irishman?
Fill his wellies full of water.

Paddy on University Challenge was asked where the Andes were and he replied, "On the end of my wrists."

Paddy, when asked what Gandhi's first name was, replied:
"Could it be Goosey Goosey?"

Paddy, when asked what hippies were, replied:
"What your leggies hang on to."

How do you define 144 Irishmen?
Gross stupidity.

Definition of an Irishman – a simple machine that converts Guinness into pee.

Heard about the Irish Humpty Dumpty?
The wall fell on him.

Heard about the Irish fish?
It drowned.

Why wasn't Jesus Christ born in Ireland?
Because they couldn't find three wise men.

Heard about the Irishman who thought that Sherlock Holmes was a block of flats?

Heard about the Irishman who thought the Ellesmere Port was a new dinner wine?

Heard about the Irishman who wanted to buy a house, so he went to British Home Stores?

Paddy's wife gave birth to triplets and now he is looking for the other two fellows!

Heard about the Irishman who thought that Sheffield Wednesday was a Bank Holiday?

Heard about the Irishman who drove his lorry off Beachy Head to test the air brakes?

Heard about the Irishman who stole a calendar? He got twelve months!

Paddy thought that Johnny Cash was change from a Durex machine!

Heard about the Irishman driving in the Indianapolis 500 and had 32 pit stops? 1 for petrol and 31 to ask the way!

Heard about the Irishman who went to the Dentist to have a wisdom tooth put in?

Heard about the Irishman who thought that Royal Enfield was where the Queen Mother kept her chickens?

Heard about the Irishman who thought that Pontious Pilot worked for Air Lingus?

Heard about the Irishman who thought that Itchy Fanny was a Japanese motor bike?

Heard about the Irishman who got a pair of water ski's for Christmas and spent a year looking for a lake with a slope?

Paddy bought a paper shop – it blew away!

Heard about the Irish Bank Teller who gave change for a fifty-three pound note?

Irish Bank Teller swallowed some money and, when his wife phoned the hospital, she was told that there was no change!

Heard about the Irishman who refused to cheque book because he didn't like the pattern!

Paddy says to Mick, "What happens if this bomb goes off in the car?" Mick says to Paddy, "Oh, it will be alright, there's another bomb in the boot."

What do you get if you cross an Irishman with a pig?
Thick bacon!

What do you call an Irish Brain Surgeon?
A Chiropodist!

What do you call an Irishman with half-a-brain?
Gifted!

What do you do when an Irishman throws a hand-grenade at you?
Pull the pin out and throw it back at him!

What do Irishmen wear in summer?
Peep-toed wellies!

What's black, shrivelled and hangs from the ceiling?
An Irish Electrician!

What do you call an Irish Frankenstein?
"Begorrah"!

How do you pick out the Irishmen on the Oil Rigs?
They're the men who are trying to feed bread to the helicopters!

How do you confuse an Irishman?
Give him twelve shovels and tell him to take his pick!

How do you make an Irishman dizzy?
Put him in a barrel and tell him to pee in the corner!

How do you tell a level-headed Irishman?
He dribbles from both sides of the mouth at the same time!

How do you get an Irishman to burn his ears?
Telephone him when he is ironing!

What do you call a pregnant Irish woman?
A dope carrier!
How do you tell an Irish Solicitor?
He wears pin-striped wellies and a donkey jacket!

Why is semen white and urine yellow?
So Paddy knows if he is coming or going!

Tourist to Irish waiter in Dublin café:
"What are the prawns like today?"

Answer: "Little Pink Fish, just like yesterday."

Heard about the Irish Sea Scout who went camping and his tent sunk?

Heard about the Irish Parachute that opens on impact?

Heard about the Irish Kamikaze pilot who is writing his memoirs?

Heard about the Irish Firing Squad, who formed a circle?

Heard about the Irish Driver who rolled forward on a hill start?

Heard about the Irish Nymphomaniac who borrowed a vibrator from Wimpey's?

Heard about the Irish tap dancer who fell in the sink?

Heard about the Irishman who hi-jacked a submarine and demanded two parachutes and £20,000 ransom?

Heard about the Irishman who kidnapped the Prime Minister and then sent him home with a ransom note?

Heard about the Irishman who crashed his helicopter?
He switched the blades off because he couldn't stand the draught.

Heard about the Irishman who won two prizes in the Generation Game? A sliding door and a conveyor belt!

Heard about the Irishman who found a milk churn in a field and thought it was a cow's nest?

Heard about the Irishman who picked his nose and took the lining out of his cap?

Heard about the Irishman who got a job sweeping up the leaves in a park and fell out of a tree and broke his leg?

Heard about the Irishman who was studying Greek Mythology and thought Satyr was Buffalo Bill?

Heard about the Irishman who bought a pair of wellies and took them back next day for a longer piece of string?

Heard about the Irishman who went for a job with Weetabix the Builders?

Heard about the Irishman who has entered the Olympics in the kneading the shot and catching the javelin?

Heard about the Irishman who bought his wife a donkey jacket because she wanted a coat made of animal skin?

HOW ABOUT AN IRISH CROSSWORD?

5 by 5 (25) SQUARES (or is that a bit too complicated?)

Clues Across:

1. Tool
2. Puppet
3. Magazine
4. Drink
5. Blow

Clues Down:

1. Vegetable
2. Sheep
3. Egg layers
4. Oceans

5. What you dropped in 3 down

THE ANSWER LOOKS LIKE THIS:

P U N C H

P U N C H

P U N C H

P U N C H

P U N C H

GOOD, AYE!

FINALLY ON THE EMERALD ISLE …

An Irishman's letter to the Family Planning Clinic:

Dear Sirs,

I wish to apply for an operation to make me sterile. My reasons are numerous and, after seven years of marriage and seven children, I have come to the conclusion that contraceptives are totally useless.

After getting married, I was advised to use the 'Rhythm Method'. Despite trying the tango and samba, my wife fell pregnant and I ruptured myself doing the cha-cha-cha!

A doctor suggested using the 'Safe Period'. At the time we were living with in-laws and we had to wait three weeks for a safe period when the house was empty. Needless to say, this did not work.

A lady of several years' experience, informed us that if we made love whilst breast-feeding we would be alright. It's hardly Newcastle Brown Ale, but I did end up with a clear skin, silky hair and felt very healthy. But my wife ended up pregnant again.

Another 'Old Wives Tale' we heard said that if my wife jumped up and down after intercourse, it would prevent pregnancy. This she did, but after constant breast-feeding my wife ended up with two black eyes and eventually knocked herself out.

So, I asked the chemist about the 'Sheath'. The chemist demonstrated how easy it was to use, so I bought a packet. My wife fell pregnant again, which did not surprise me. I fail to see how a Durex stretched over the thumb, as the chemist showed me, can prevent babies.

She was then supplied with the coil and, after several unsuccessful attempts to fit it, we realised that we had got a left-hand thread and my wife is definitely a right-hand screw.

The 'Dutch Cap' came next. We were very hopeful of this as it did not interfere with our sex life at all. But, alas, it did give my wife several headaches. We were given the largest available, but it was still too tight across her forehead.

You must appreciate my problem.

At present we have reverted to 'Oral Sex' but, as you will agree, just talking about it is no substitute for the real thing.

Yours desperately.

-6-

The World of Sex: How to Kill an Eel & other Tales

WHICH BRINGS US TO A LETTER FROM 'MAYFAIR'
CENTREFOLD …

Dear Sir,

Your name has been submitted to us with your full frontal photograph;
I regret to inform you that we will be unable to use your body in our
centrefold this month.

On a scale of 0–10 your body was rated -2 by our panel of women
judges, ranging in age from 50–70 years. We tried to assemble a panel
in the age bracket of 25–45 years, but we could not get them to stop
laughing long enough to reach a decision.

Should, however, the tastes of the American woman ever change so
drastically that bodies such as yours would be appreciated in our
Mayfair Centrefold, you will be notified by this office immediately. In
the meantime, don't call us – we'll call you!

However, may we just add that our panel did commend you for your
unusual pose. Were you wounded in the War, or do you ride a bike a
lot?

Yours sympathetically,
Editor, Mayfair Centrefold

HOW ABOUT SOME LOVE LETTERS?

A … is for apple, and Adam as well, the fruit of the fall, and the fellow
who fell.

B ... is for buttocks so fine and so clean, and also the bugger who gets in between.

C ... is the cunt that is covered with hair, and the cock that insists upon getting his share.

D ... is for dirty, the jokes that are rife, as well as the dustman who dong's up your wife.

E ... is for easy, the girl who is that ... one who will screw at the drop of a hat.

F ... is for fart that you blow in the bog or, if you are elsewhere, it must be the dog.

G ... is the girl who will look in your eye, and say that she doesn't but still she might try.

H ... is the horn that awakened John Peel, and frightened his wife when she came for a feel.

I ... is the icy and innocent miss, whose thing is inactive except for a piss.

J ... is the joy that you feel when you screw, with a girl who is pretty and randy and new.

K ... is the king who is shagging his queen with a crown on his willie – it's a sight to be seen.

L ... is for lesbian who can't be a man, so she uses a dildo and does what she can.

M ... is the menstrual flow you deplore, 'til you roll the girl over and try the back door.

N ... is for ninety and also nineteen, and the nookie you get in the years in between.

O ... is the orifice all men adore, and the subject of books about what it is for.

P ... is for prick that's a hot tip to back, he'll win by a length at the sniff of a crack.

Q ... is the quim that you're longing to feel; for the whore it's the ticket that brings her next meal.

R ... is the randiest of rams to be blunt, from the cradle to the grave it's on with the hunt.

S ... is the safety girls feel on the pill, and the spunk it allows them to take with a will.

T ... is for tits but if she had none at all, she can get a new silicone pair installed.

U ... is the unbridled delight of the wench, when she grips like a vice on the carpenter's bench.

V ... is for virgin who wants you to come, she'll deny you her fanny and offer her bum.

W ... is the dream that's exciting and wet, it's hell on the sheets but it's not a bad bet.

X ... is the great unattainable X, the girl you can't have and the pride of her sex.

Y ... is the yawning magnificent slit, that is faithfully yours when you fancy a bit.

Z ... is for zoo where the monkeys are frank, and show you six ways of having a spank.

But S E and X – the best letters of all, have been with mankind since the time of the fall!

HERE IS A NICE LITTLE QUIZ – GET YOUR FRIENDS TO WRITE THEIR ANSWERS ON A PIECE OF PAPER …

1. Are you glad to be alive?
2. Have you a happy disposition?
3. Give a boys/girls name.
4. How long does it take you to walk a mile?
5. Write down any number up to 10.
6. Do you drink much?
7. Write down any number up to 15.
8. What is your favourite meat?
9. What is your favourite colour?
10. Do you wear suspenders?
11. What do you think of the weather?

NOW GET THEM TO ANSWER THESE QUESTIONS, USING THEIR PREVIOUS ANSWERS …

1. Do you like it?
2. Do you get it?
3. Who from?
4. How long for?
5. How often a week?
6. Are you satisfied?
7. How many inches have you got?
8. What does it look like?
9. What colour is it?
10. Would you change it?
11. How do you feel after it?

SHOULD CAUSE A FEW LAUGHS!

HERE ARE 35 REASONS WHY
MEN ARE BETTER THAN CUCUMBERS …

1. Cucumbers might be big, but it's boring watching them grow.
2. Who wants indigestion five times a week?
3. Only a contortionist could manage 69 with a cucumber!
4. You don't get slugs with a willy.
5. You won't choke on the pips.
6. Cucumbers fall into pieces when you roll back the skin!
7. Cucumbers might be less fattening, but you can't beat meat and
   two veg!
8. Cucumbers might be satisfying, but try making up a foursome!
9. If a cucumber throbs, it might be full of maggots.
10. If you want to take it easy, a cucumber won't do it for you.
11. Who ever heard of a cucumber with a tongue?
12. Big girls don't lose their man half-way through.
13. If you fancy a group session you can only hold two cucumbers.
14. Cucumbers won't get up and turn the light off afterwards.
15. There's no variety with a cucumber!
16. Cucumbers can't mend fuses.
17. If the milkman gets too amorous, you will look bloody
    silly threatening to tell your cucumber!
18. You can eat a cucumber, but they can't eat you!
19. If you're into love bites, you've got to hit yourself damn hard with
    a cucumber to get a bruise.
20. You're really into a problem if you like bondage!
21. You could have a job to reach if you're on all fours!
22. A cucumber never whispers sweet nothings, i.e. "Come on, sit
    on my face!"
23. Cucumbers break if you slip out and stub them on your nut hole!
24. You can't buy happy hats to fit a cucumber!
25. Cucumbers won't fetch a tissue and clean you up!
26. If you want a divorce, any man's worth more than a
    soiled cucumber!
27. A cucumber doesn't say sorry if it hurts.

28. With a cucumber, who's going to hold your ankles round your ears!
29. Cucumbers don't fart but, by Christ, they stink when they start to rot.
30. If it's a bad summer, there are still plenty of hard full-size willies.
31. When you've finished with a cucumber it doesn't shrink back to a handy size.
32. You don't get the satisfaction of hearing a cucumber groan!
33. Cucumbers cost money, we don't charge (see you later).
34. Who wants a cucumber without salad cream!
35. If you suffer from dry hair you get no help from a cucumber!

P.S. By the way ... what does a man suffering from DIPHALLIC TERATA have?

Two Penises!

BIONIC FRED

Now this is the tale of young Freddie Law,
Whose sexual equipment got jammed in the door.
By the time they had freed him, he didn't feel well,
His poor private parts were mangled to hell.

They rushed him to hospital, the ambulance flew,
But when they arrived there was nowt they could do.
What a bad blow for Fred, condemned without choice
To a life without sex and a high squeaky voice.

But lucky for Fred, so he wouldn't feel a fool,
Some bright spark suggested a bionic tool.
A smart new electric one made out of brass,
Though the batteries would have to be kept up his arse.

Now newly equipped and after a rest,
Fred thought he would put his tool to the test.
So finding a woman, the nearest one handy,

Supplied her with drink and made her feel randy.

She, without waiting, put her hand in Fred's flies,
When she felt what was there gave a cry of surprise.
"That's my bionic chopper, now let's have some fun!"
"Cor Blimey!" she said. "It felt more like a gun."

They both stripped off quick and Fred entered fast,
Then he turned up the speed knob and gave her full blast.
They clung to each other as Fred's dick shook some more,
Then they bounced off the bed and rolled onto the floor.

How the pace hotted up and they started to choke
As the air in the room became filled with blue smoke.
With a bang, Fred's left bollock flew into the air –
And his other went bonkerty-bonk down the stair.

Then back for repair went poor Fred full of woe,
Was this how his sex life was destined to go?
To return to his doctor at the end of each shag
With his prick in his pocket and his balls in a bag.

But they fixed up young Fred, made him manly again
And they replaced the batteries with a flex to the main.
So, if he can't get a girl now, lucky Fred doesn't cry,
'Cause he's now AC/DC and can go with a guy.

Dear Wife,

During the last year, I tried to make love to you 365 times. I
succeeded 36 times, which is an average of once every ten days. The
following is a list of reasons why I did not succeed more often:

1. We will wake up the children   17 times
2. It's too late   15 times

3. I'm too tired	5 times
4. It's too early	52 times
5. It's too hot	15 times
6. Pretending to be asleep	49 times
7. Windows open, neighbours will hear	9 times
8. Backache	2 times
9. Headache	16 times
10. Sunburn	10 times
11. Your mother will hear us	6 times
12. Not in the mood	21 times
13. We will wake the baby	17 times
14. Want to watch late tv show	7 times
15. Too sore	9 times
16. Will spoil new hair-do	4 times
17. Wrong time of month	4 times
18. You had to go to the toilet	9 times

During the 36 times I did succeed, the activity was not entirely satisfactory, because 6 times you just laid there, 8 times you reminded me there was a crack in the ceiling, 14 times you told me to hurry up and get it over with, 7 times I had to wake you up to tell you I had finished, and once I thought I had hurt you because I felt you move.

Dear Husband,

I think you have things a little confused. Here are the real reasons you did not get more than you did:

1. Came home drunk and tried to stuff the cat	7 times
2. Didn't come home at all	29 times
3. Didn't come	14 times
4. Came too soon	26 times
5. Went soft before you got it in	18 times
6. Cramp in toes	9 times
7. Working late	49 times
8. Said you had a rash, probably from a toilet seat	21 times

9. In a fight, someone kicked you in the balls　　　4 times
10. Caught it in your zip　　　　　　　　　　　　6 times
11. Got a cold – your nose keeps running　　　　14 times
12. Brewers droop　　　　　　　　　　　　　95 times
13. Your tea was too hot you burnt your tongue　　9 times
14. You had a splinter in your finger　　　　　　4 times
15. Lost the notion after thinking of it all day　　18 times
16. Came in your pyjamas while reading a dirty book　8 times

Of the times we did get together, the reason I did lay still was because you had missed and was stuffing the sheet. I wasn't talking about the crack in the ceiling, what I said was: "Would you prefer me on my back or kneeling?" The time you felt me move was because you had farted and I was trying to breathe. However, 6 months ago, I phoned Alcoholics Anonymous for help and their representative has been calling and keeping me happy.

HOW TO KILL AN EEL

Little Johnny was only 11 years old and, like most boys of his age, rather curious. He had been hearing quite a lot about courting from older boys and had been wondering what it was and how it was done. One day he asked his mother, who became rather flustered and, instead of explaining things to him, she told him to hide behind the curtains and watch his older sister and her boyfriend. This he did and the following morning he described everything he saw to his mother.

"Sis and her boyfriend sat talking for a while, then he turned off the light and they started kissing and hugging. I figured she must be getting sick because her face started looking funny. I guess he must have thought so too because he put his hand up her blouse to feel her heart, just like a doctor. Only he's not as smart as the doctor because he seemed to have trouble finding her heart.

"I guess he was getting pretty sick too, because soon both of them started panting and getting out of breath. His other hand must have been getting cold, because he put it under her skirt. About this time, Sis got worse and began to moan and sigh and squirm around and slide down to the end of the sofa. This is when the fever started. I know it was a fever, because Sis told him she felt really hot. This was when I realised what was making them sick … a big eel had got in his pants somehow. It jumped out of his hand and stood there, about 10 inches long. Then he grabbed it with one hand to stop it getting away.

"When Sis saw it, she got really scared; her eyes got wide and her mouth fell open. Sis started calling out "God" and things like that. She said it was the biggest one she had ever seen. (I should show her the ones at the lake, they're much bigger). Anyway, she got brave and tried to kill the eel by biting its head off. All of a sudden, she made a noise and let it go … I guess it bit her back. Then she grabbed it with both hands and held it tight, while he took a muzzle out of his pocket and slipped it over the eels head to stop it biting again.

"Sis laid back and opened her legs so she could get it in a scissor lock. He helped her by laying on top of the eel. The eel put up a fight. Sis started groaning and her boyfriend almost ripped up the couch. I guess they wanted to kill the eel between them.

"After a while they both stopped moaning and gave a great sigh. Her boyfriend got up and, sure enough, they had killed the eel. I knew it was dead, because it was just hanging there limp and some of its sides were hanging out. Sis and her boyfriend were a little tired after the battle but soon went back courting again. He started kissing and hugging her again and, by golly, the eel wasn't dead! It jumped straight up and started to fight again. I guess eels have nine lives, like cats.

"This time Sis jumped up and tried to kill the eel by sitting on it. Finally, after 35 minutes, I knew it was dead because I saw Sis's boyfriend peel its skin off and flush it down the toilet."

ERNIE

You can hear his knackers pound as he raced across the ground,
The clatter of his prick as it swung around and around.
As he galloped into Market Street, he had no pants or vest –
His name was Ernie and he had the biggest chopper in the west.

Now Ernie laid a widow, a lady known as Sue,
She said she'd like to try it – he said, "I bet you do!"
She said she was too big for him cos she had it twice a week,
So Ernie smashed his chopper across her great big cheek.

Now Ernie had a rival, an evil looking man,
Called One-Ball Ted from Teddington, he drove the Durex van.
He tempted her with Featherlight and got his end away –
All Ernie had to offer, was her oats three times a day.

One day, Ted saw Ernie's car outside her door …
It drove him mad to find it still there at half-past four.
Poor Ted, he could not stand it, it made him very sick,
So he smashed all Ernie's windows with a great big mucky brick.

So Ernie ran outside, his eyes fixed on the brick,
They stood there face to face and Ted went for his prick.
But Ernie was too fast for him, it wasn't what was planned …
And a hairy sweaty ball sent it spinning from his hand.

Sue ran between the both of them to keep them far apart,
But Ernie said, "Push off, you silly looking tart!"
And, as he looked up in utter and sheer disgust,
A size ten ball hit him and Ernie bit the dust.

Ernie was only twenty and didn't want to die,
But now he's laying women in that brothel in the sky.
There isn't any virgins left, he's had them all by force …
And the 'syph' he had in his balls has gone from bad to worse.

But a woman's needs are many – so Sue, she slept with Ted,
But a strange thing happened on that night as Ted laid her in the bed.
Was that the trees a-rustling or maybe even more …
Like Ernie's ghostly chopper a-banging on the door?

They'll never forget Ernie – the biggest in the West!

NEW INSTRUCTIONS FOR DARLING (DIALING)
BRITISH TELECOM STD LETTER-DIAL TELEPHONE

Instructions for using the New Dial Telephone:

On the telephone there is a dial with letters to indicate the exchange wanted. For instance, S is for South, P is for Portobello or Pussy if using the phonetic code, or O for Operator.

If South is required, put your finger in the S hole. If Portobello is wanted put your finger in the P hole (or the Pussy, according to your requirements) and if the Operator is wanted, put your finger in the Operator's hole until she comes, then she will give you the required connections.

If you have fingered the P hole or the Operator's hole correctly, you should hear a soft purring sound. Should you have inserted your finger in the wrong hole, the R's hole for instance, you will hear a high-pitched scream. In this event, discontinue using your finger and put the end of your pencil in Pussy. When you finish, you may find that the Operator has lost her ring.

Special Information:
Foreign calls may be made by dialling F, but the girl may request you to use another letter, usually a French one, in addition to the normal procedure.

General Information:
In certain cases, satisfactory connections may prove to be impossible.

This could be due to: (a) two or more subscribers fingering the Operator's hole at the same time, or (b) the cable engineers have slipped a length into the Operator's socket. You will have to wait for service until the Engineer has removed his tool.

To remedy the above faults:
(a) Hold your instrument tightly round the middle with your left hand and feel underneath the bottom with your right hand until the Operator responds.
(b) Remove your finger from either the P hole or the R's hole, grasp the flex and pull your wire until you hear a buzzing in your ear.

POST OFFICE TELECOMMUNICATIONS?

TIME FOR SOME MORE DEFINITIONS …

Mothers Day	Nine months after Fathers day.
Brassiere	Device for making mountains out of mole hills.
Adultery	The wrong people doing the right things.
Divorce	When two people cannot stomach each other.
Kiss	An application at headquarters for a job at base.
Kissing	Sabotage before invasion.
Mistress	Something between Master and mattress.
Prostitute	Busy Body.
Rape	Seduction without salesmanship.
Twins	Womb mates that later become bosom pals.
Virgin	A wise crack.
Pyjamas	Article placed in bed in case of fire.
Board of Trade	Bench in Hyde Park.
Naval Cutter	The elastic in knickers.
Grub Screw	Sexual intercourse during the lunch hour.
Sand Bag	Desert prostitute.
Love	A fellow feeling.
Jealousy	Another fellow feeling.
Puff Adder	A man who blows off in the bath and counts the bubbles.

Alimony	The screw you don't get for the screw you got.
Taxidermist	A man who mounts animals.
Yankee Clipper	An American Rabbi.
Virgin Sheep	One that can run faster than the shepherd.
Endless Belt	A sailor on 24 hours leave.
Ball Race	Tom cat with 20 yards start on vet.
Wind Jammer	A hard turd with a knot in it.
Blunder Bus	A coach load of spinsters going to a Maternity Home.
Hormone	Noise heard outside a brothel.
Apprehension	The first time you realise that you can't do it the first time.
Fear	The second time you realise that you can't do it the first time.
Homosexuality	The means to widen the circle of one's friends.
Panic	Two sailors in the shower with the soap on the floor.
Insomnia	When the bridegroom cannot get off to sleep.
Lady	One who doesn't smoke, drink, or swear when it slips out.
Pansy	One who likes his vice-versa.
Private Secretary	A good one who never misses a period.
Sob Sister	One who sits on your knee and bawls and makes it hard for you.
Welsh Rabbit	Cardiff Virgin.
Spring Fever	When the blood of a young man's veins turns to lead in his pencil.
Housewife	A gadget you screw on the bed.

AND HERE'S A GOOD HOME-COOKING RECIPE …

BANANA BREAD

Ingredients and Utensils:
2 laughing eyes

2 loving arms
2 well-shaped legs
2 milk containers
1 fur-lined mixing bowl
1 large banana

Mixing Instructions:
1. Look into laughing eyes.
2. Spread well-shaped legs slowly.
3. Squeeze and massage milk containers very gently, until fur-lined bowl is well greased.
4. Add banana and gently work in and out until well-creamed.
5. Cover with nuts and sigh with relief.

NOTE: Bread is done when banana is soft. Be sure to wash mixing utensils and do not lick bowl.

ATTENTION: If bread starts to rise ... leave town!

THE GOOD FOOD GUIDE TO CHINESE DELICACIES ...

Meat Dishes:
1. Bol Oxs — Hot meat balls
2. Sur Kum Sihz — Sausage slices
3. Hol Mein Kok — Scrag end encased in ladyfingers
4. Kor Sor — Rolled pork fillets rubbed in Chilli powder
5. Eja Ku Lait — Shaft of mutton in white cream sauce
6. Long Dik — Coq in van
7. Veri Ti Rin — Massive extrusion of forcemeat

Vegetables:
8. Wan Kin — Bamboo shoots
9. Pei Sof — Chinese leaves
10. Wot Kung Fu Dat — Tossed salad

11. Sik in Lu	Sweet and sour in hot sauce
12. Pu Bik	Young sprouts
13. Sik In Lu	Extra number 11
14. Du Reks	Entre coat
15. Hoo Pong In Car See	Yellow rice with meat droppings
16. Hoo Kum On Mat	Thick white rice on rye bread

Sauces:

17. Pei Sol	Cantonese drippings
18. Sei Men Drip	Delicately flavoured white sauce
19. Yu Kum	Hot custard
20. Hu Lade Turd	Brown sauce with nuts
21. Fan Tom Ar Sol	Invisible brown sauce without nuts

Specialties:

22. Lik Mein	Plate of the day
23. Fug Yu	Chinese toast
24. Munth Lei	Popular dish of the period
25. Kow Poo	Savoury pancakes
26. Doggie Bag	Chinese takeaway
27. Ho Mo	Sausage surprise
28. Bo Gee	Pick of the week

Desserts:

29. Vee Dee	Spotted dick
30. Kum In Yu	Cream squirt
31. Yu Pong	Crap suzette
32. Kum Lots	Extra portion cream
33. Ars Pik	Chocolate fingers
34. Hoo Shat In Fann	Chocolate spread
35. Or Jee	Chinese stuffing on a bed of mandarins
36. Es Kie Mo Kum	Frosted banana cream
37. Tu Tun On Goo Lies	Crushed nuts
38. Wun Hung Low	Mixed nuts
39. Di Rere	Chinese afters in aromatic brown sauce
40. Hu Pong	Chinese snifters

41. Kwik Wank   Cream slice

Beverages:
42. Yu Rine   Jasmine tea
43. Wob Li Tit   Milk shake

HOW ABOUT THE FOLLOWING SONNET TO A TIN OF CORNED BEEF?

O toothsome cube, thou tit-bit, glistening red
Here flecked, there flecked, with snowy streaks of gristle
Bespeaking tasteful power, what mem'ries bristle,
In ev'ry oz, the cow in which you bred
That peer'mid kine,with what proud measured tread
She tinwards steered, alfalfa and sweet thistle
Cud to the last brave vitamin, let my pen chisel
Naughty but pye praise for each and every shred.

All hail to thee in rissoles of all sizes
All hail to thee in similar disguises
The food of fighters, yea of non-combs
Thou hast paved airfields wast employed as bombs,
Thou art my friend, indeed, and yet my grief,
I honour thee, and hate thy guts, Corned Beef.

REPORT FROM THE HOLIDAY ...

(please tick as applicable)

Dear ....

I'm having a wonderful time.
Wish you could be here with me to enjoy:
The Scenery ..… The Night Life ..... The Sex Life .....

The food is: Delicious ….. Synthetic ….. Pig Swill …..
Last night we had: Pheasant Under Glass …..
Seaweed Soup ….. Mud-flaps Flambe …..
So much for my diet!

And you wouldn't believe the prices – £5 for a:
Wrist Watch ….. Plastic Flamingo ….. Lava Lamp …..
I found it hard to resist.

The people here are really:
Friendly ….. Obese ….. Forward …..
Yesterday a man walked right up to me and said:
Hello ….. Say Melancholy Baby ….. Flashed …..

The weather has been:
Beautiful ….. Unpredictable ….. The Pits …..
But we're expecting:
A Rainstorm ….. A Snowstorm ….. A Nuclear Holocaust …..

Well, I have to sign off now – we're going to visit:
A Snake Farm ….. A Kazoo Factory …..
The Birthplace of Angela Rippon …..
Some opportunities come along just once in a lifetime.

Your: Friend ….. Folks ….. Turn …..

P.S. Give my best to:
The Gang ….. The Queen ….. and Whatshisname …..

A YOUNG MAN'S LAMENT

When I was young and full of life,
I thought I'd like to be
With other fellows in the town
And go out on the spree.

So in the evening I prepared
It was my full intent
I wandered down the busy street
And on the spree I went.

I hadn't gone so very far
When to my great delight,
I met a girl I'd known for years
And with her spent the night.
We talked of everything we knew
About the facts of life,
And in the morning as I left
She said she'd be my wife.

Chorus:
Oh, it's coming up by degrees
It's coming up by degrees,
We've got the table and the chair
We've got the baby's underwear.
We've got the bar of soap
To wash the baby's knees,
We haven't got the baby yet
But it's coming by degrees.

I hurried to my parents' home
My mother said to me
"Where have you been? For I have seen
You have not slept in bed."
I said I'd met a friend of mine
Who once thought I'd wed,
Excitement proved too much for her
She took me home to bed.

Chorus

Now Father he was very grave
And said to me with scorn,

Now don't forget – you will regret
The day that you were born.
I heeded not my Fathers words
But went my own sweet way,
And straightway to her parents went
To fix the wedding day.

Chorus

Arrangements then were quickly made
And friends were notified,
When gathered round the wedding spread
They looked on me with pride.
And having satisfied their fill
Their homeward way to wend,
We hurried off to catch the train,
Our honeymoon to spend.

Chorus

The first night of our honeymoon
I jumped into the bed,
I put my arms around her waist
And this is what she said.
"Oh, take away your tickling arm
You know it's all in vain,
For if you don't – I really won't
Walk out with you again."

Chorus

As time went on, I plainly seen
My wife was growing pale,
The stress and strain of married life
Began to tell its tale.
Until one day the nurse came in,
She said forget past sins

And hurry to the chemist shop
For napkins and some pins.

Chorus

Now wheel the perambulator, John,
And wheel it very slow.
Mind the child – don't get wild,
Be careful as you go.
And when you reach the corner, John,
Before you cross the road,
Just lift your front wheels up a bit
And don't forget your load.

Chorus

Now, you young men all heed my tale
Before you go too far,
When on the brink – just stop to think
What fools we fellows are.
These women are such fickle things,
Just leave them high and dry
For goodness sake, pray you don't make
The same mistakes as I!

Chorus

AS COLD AS:

As cold as the rocks on an ice-bound pool,
As cold as the tip of an Eskimo's tool,
As cold as an icicle all glossy and glum,
As cold as the fringe 'round a polar bear's bum,
As cold as charity (and that's bloody chilly) …
But not as cold as our poor Willy – he's dead!

IF YOU ARE UNHAPPY …

Once upon a time, there was a non-conforming sparrow who decided not to fly south for the winter. However, soon the weather turned so cold that he reluctantly started to fly south. In a short time, ice began to form on his wings and he fell to earth in a barnyard, almost frozen. A cow passed by and crapped on the little sparrow. The sparrow thought it was the end. But the manure warmed him and defrosted his wings. Warm and happy, able to breathe, he started to sing. Just then a large cat came by and, hearing the chirping, investigated the sounds. The cat cleared away the manure, found the chirping bird and promptly ate him.

THE MORAL OF THE STORY …

1. Everyone who shits on you is not necessarily your enemy.

2. Everyone who gets you out of the shit is not necessarily your friend.

   P..And, if you're warm and happy in a pile of shit … keep your mouth SHUT!

AND SO TO OUR AMERICAN FRIENDS … COMMUNICATION!

OPERATION HALLEY'S COMET:

A Colonel in the USAF issued the following directive to his Executive Officers:

Tomorrow evening, at approximately 2000 hours, Halley's Comet will be visible in this area, an event which only occurs once every 75 years. Have the men fall out in the battalion area in fatigues, and I will explain this rare phenomenon to them. In case of rain, we will not be able to see anything, so assemble the men in the theatre and I will show them a film of it.

Executive Officer to Squadron Commander:
By order of the Colonel, tomorrow at 2000 hours, Halley's Comet will appear above the battalion area. If it rains, fall the men out in fatigues, then march to the theatre, where this phenomenon will take place, something which occurs only once every 75 years.

Squadron Leader to Lieutenant:
By order of the Colonel in fatigues at 2000 hours tomorrow evening, the phenomenal Halley's Comet will appear in the theatre. In case of rain in the battalion area, the Colonel will give another order, something which occurs once every 75 years.

Lieutenant to Sergeant:
Tomorrow at 2000 hours, the Colonel will appear in the theatre with Halley's Comet, something which happens every 75 years. If it rains, the Colonel will order the Comet into the battalion area.

Sergeant to Squad:
When it rains tomorrow at 2000 hours, the phenomenal 75-year old General Halley, accompanied by the Colonel will drive his Comet through the battalion area in fatigues.

IN THE POST OFFICE ALSO –

AN ILLUSTRATION OF A COMMUNICATION PROBLEM …

Regional Director to all Head Postmasters:
Tomorrow morning there will be a total eclipse of the sun at 9.00. This is something we cannot see happen every day, so arrange for your staff to attend (being a Sunday, appropriate pay rates will apply) in their best clothes to watch it. To mark this extremely rare occurrence, I will see that you receive my personal explanation so that you may describe it to all present in detail. If it is raining, we shall not be able to see it very well and, in that case, the staff should assemble in the sorting office.

Head Postmaster to Assistant Head Postmaster:
By order of the Regional Director there will be a total eclipse of the sun at 9.00 tomorrow morning, Sunday. If it is raining we shall not be able to see it very well on site, in our best clothes. In that case the disappearance of the sun will be followed through in the sorting office. This is something that we cannot see happen every day.

Assistant Head Postmaster to Officer in Charge of Sorting Office:
By order of the Regional Director we shall follow through in our best clothes, the disappearance of the sun in the sorting office at 9.00 tomorrow, Sunday morning. The Head Postmaster will tell us if it's going to rain. This is something which we cannot see happen every day.

Officer in Charge to Supervisor:
If it is raining in the sorting office tomorrow morning which is something we cannot see happening every day, our Regional Director, in his best clothes, will disappear at 9.00.

Supervisor to Postmen:
Tomorrow morning at 9.00 our Regional Director will disappear. It's a pity that we cannot see this happening every day!

AND WITH THE POST OFFICE IN MIND –

TO SOME LETTERS …

Here is a copy of a letter from an Australian farmer in response to an Income Tax demand:

Dear Sirs,

Your heated letter arrived this morning in an unsealed envelope with a penny stamp on it. My son and I derived much pleasure from it.

You say you thought the account could have been settled long ago and cannot understand why: well, here are the reasons.

In 1954 I bought a small sawmill on credit, in 1955 I bought a team of horses, two ponies, a timber wagon, a double-barrelled shot gun and two razor-backed pigs, all on credit. In 1956, the bloody mill burned down to the ground leaving not a damned thing. One of my ponies died and I loaned the other to a stupid bastard who starved the poor bugger to death. Then I joined the Church in 1957, my father died and my brother was hanged for raping a pensioner, a tramp seduced my daughter and I had to pay the man $50 to prevent him becoming a relative.

In 1958, my boy got mumps which spread to his balls and the lad had to be castrated to save his life. Later, I went fishing and the rotten boat overturned drowning two of my boys (neither being the one who was castrated). In 1959, my wife ran away with the shepherd and left me with twins as a souvenir.

I employed a housekeeper and later married her to keep expenses down. I had a hell of a job trying to get her pregnant, I saw a doctor who advised me to create some excitement at the crucial moment. That night, I took a shotgun to be with me and at the time I thought was right I leaned out of the window and fired the gun. Result – the wife soiled the bed! I ruptured myself and shot the best cow I ever owned.

In 1960, some joker cut the nuts off my prize bull. I took to drink; I carried on drinking until I had nothing left but a pocket watch and a weak bladder. Winding the watch and running for a wee kept me busy for a time. After a year I took heart and bought a manure spreader, reaper, a binder and a car – all on credit. My new wife got VD from a salesman, and another son died (not the one who was castrated) – he had wiped his bottom on a poisoned rabbit skin and, from the infection – he died.

You can imagine my delight upon reading that you will cause 'trouble' if I should not pay up. If you can think of any trouble I have missed, I should be glad to hear about it. Trying to get money out of me is like trying to poke a pound of butter up a porcupine's arse with a red-hot needle!

I am praying that a shower of skunk shit will pass your way and hope the centre of it falls square over the bunch of bastards in your office who sent me the final demand!

Yours.

BUT HAVE YOU READ THIS ONE?

THE REVEREND HAROLD KNIGHT, THE RESCUE MISSION, 182 ELLIOT STREET, LONDON SW1

Dear,

Perhaps you have heard of me and my nationwide campaign in the cause of temperance. Each year for the past fourteen, I have made a tour of Wales and the South of England, including Gravesend, Maidstone, Dover, Sevenoaks and your area, and have delivered a series of lectures on the evils of drinking.

On this tour I have been accompanied by a young friend and assistant – James Woodward. James, a young man of good family and excellent background, is a pathetic example of a life ruined by excessive indulgence in alcohol and women.

James would appear with me at the lectures and sit on the platform, wheezing and staring at the audience through bleary, bloodshot eyes, sweating profusely, picking his nose, passing wind and making obscene gestures, while I would point him out as an example of what drinking, etc can do to a person.

Last summer, unfortunately, he died. A mutual friend has given me your name and I wondered if you would care to take James' place on my next tour?

Yours in faith,

Rev Harold Knight
Rescue Mission

P.S. I will actually be on tour during the next couple of weeks, preaching round St. Tropez in Southern France but, should you wish to apply for this position, please drop a note outlining why you think you would be good for this job, to one of my faithful disciples of the mission ******** ******* at the Marks Tey Hotel, where she is currently carrying out a very successful mission with the aid of a parrot!

AND THERE IS ALWAYS …

THE INTERNATIONAL COUNCIL OF FRIENDSHIP

Dear

As part of our fostering greater world understanding, the above council has selected your home to further the Council's aims. You will be pleased to know that we have invited a family of Ugandan Asians to be guests in your home for the next four months.

This period of time will allow them to adapt themselves to our way of life, which I am sure you will appreciate. These people have suffered great social upheaval and physical privation and we will be grateful if you will do everything in your power to make their stay in your home as pleasant as possible. This will mean re-organising your home and personal habits to make them feel at home and comfortable.

The family we have selected to stay with you are called Gujeratisind and consists of the father, his two wives, seven children, one wife's brother, the father's grandparents and a Brahmin Bull. These bulls are classified as sacred beasts and thus it will be necessary for you to approach the local authority for accommodation for this animal: a heated garage will be ideal. Its food consists of pampas grass and rice. We trust this will not be too expensive for you to cope with but, unfortunately, all the Gujeratisinds are on Social Security and we will be grateful if you can give them pocket money from time to time. One important point here: the animal droppings are to remain where they fall for a minimum of 72 hours to avoid upsetting the religious feelings of the Asians. To aid you in feeding this family, we are forwarding to you 8 cwt of curry powder and chapatis and 6 cwt of dried stockfish, together with a booklet entitled 'Causes and Cures for Enteric and Dysentery Ailment' should any of them become ill.

A booklet of Urdu and Hindi phrases for everyday use will also be provided.

Examples are as follows:

Urdu or Hindi	English Translation
Naya desai Bhutto	Please change my underpants.
Hapa sesma gurulu jinti muudo jama	The lavatory is blocked and will you dig it out?
Gaja mean 109rahmin nestra	The bull is asleep on your bed.

We shall give you seven days' notice of the arrival date of the family and will be grateful if you will arrange the necessary documentation so that the family can obtain their rightful amounts of Social Security, Supplementary Benefit and Free National Health Treatment. I hope you will find this experience an interesting and rewarding, social and cultural one and make this family one of your own.

Yours sincerely,

Jitendra Patel
Cultural Rehabilitation Officer
Slappit and Daubit

BUT, BACK TO THE ESSENTIAL SERVICES …

If you think you've got troubles, read on!

Accident Report:

My Branch Secretary asked me to write down the events which led to my accident.

On the 31st December we were working on the Elmsford Village Green manhole. I had just finished the joint and was standing on the step of the van lighting a cigarette. My lighter flame flared up and I lost my balance and fell off the step. I fell on the end of a punner which was resting on my willie and twisted my left ankle. The punner twirled in the air and struck Mr Smith, the Technical Inspector, on the head as he was lifting the manhole cover with Mr Jones his assistant. Mr Smith dropped his end of the manhole cover on my right foot which broke my big and second toe.

My cries brought Mr Stacey from the van and he lifted the end of the man-hole cover. As soon as I was free, I stepped back and fell down the open manhole, suffering severe laceration of the left leg and a cut on my head which needed four stitches.

I climbed out of this manhole and, by now, I was feeling a little dazed. I stumbled over Mr Stacey, who was leaning over Mr Jones trying to revive him. I fell forward on to the gas burner which was boiling water for tea. My trousers caught fire and I could not beat out the flames. At this point, I lost my head. I limped to the nearby pond and flung myself in. As I entered the pond my right leg caught in an old bedstead which was resting on the bottom. I suffered a fracture of the right tibula. The pond was deeper than it appeared and, as I cannot swim, I commenced to drown.

Mr Jones saw my difficulty and jumped in the pond also catching his foot on the bedstead, fracturing his left ankle. He managed to hold me up and shouted for Mr Smith: unfortunately, Mr Smith was at that time unconscious, as when I had knocked him over Mr Stacey he had caught his head on the corner of the van. Eventually a passer-by helped the two of us out of the pond, called an ambulance and took us to hospital.

I have been unable to obtain any statements from the other members of the gang, as they have refused to speak to me since the accident. After 26 weeks in hospital, I have now returned to light duties.

I wish to know if I can claim compensation and if I am entitled to an allowance, as the three junior men who worked with me have now been promoted since my accident. Should I also give up smoking?

P.LUGG
Technical Electrician

NOW HERE'S AN INTER-DEPARTMENTAL CONFRONTATION …

From: The Postmaster
To: Mr Blogg, Postman Driver

I have received a letter from Mrs Smith of 12 High Road in which she states she has discovered in her coal shed, buried under 5 cwt of coal, a parcel dated 17th December. As you were the delivery officer in that area on this date, a statement regarding this is required.

To the Postmaster:
In reply to your letter, to the best of my knowledge, I have never at any time buried a parcel under 5 cwt of coal in Mrs Smith's coal shed.
Sam Bloggs

From the Postmaster:
It was not intended to imply that you were responsible for burying a parcel under 5 cwt of coal in Mrs Smith's coal shed. I merely stated that the parcel was discovered under 5 cwt of coal. I am anxious to discover how this happened. Will you therefore let me have a statement?

To the Postmaster:
I am as puzzled as you, Sir. I spent the whole of last evening in my own coal shed, trying to find out how anyone could discover anything buried under 5 cwt of coal.
Sam Bloggs.

From the Postmaster:
It is perfectly obvious that Mrs Smith did not discover the parcel buried under 5 cwt of coal, but only after removing the coal. Will you explain how the parcel came to be in the coal shed in the first place?

To the Postmaster:
Thank you for your letter of explanation. It would now appear that Mrs Smith must have known of the existence of the parcel, otherwise she would hardly have gone to the trouble of removing 5 cwt of coal.
Sam Bloggs

From the Postmaster:
For your information, Mrs Smith removed the 5 cwt of coal in the normal process of burning it and did not, as you appear to think, remove it for the express purpose of finding out what lay beneath it. Mr Bloggs, did you or did you not leave a parcel in Mrs Smith's coal shed on or about 20th December?

To the Postmaster:
In the course of my duties I handle approximately 200 parcels a week. Therefore, I am afraid I cannot remember a specific parcel after a period of time. Could you please give me further details?
Sam Bloggs

From the Postmaster:
I do not consider it necessary at this stage to give you details of the said parcel. I merely wish is to ascertain whether or not you left a parcel in Mrs Smith's coal shed on or about the given date?

To the Postmaster:
During the course of my duties, which cover four walks, I visit more than 1,000 houses, all of which I assume have coal sheds. Therefore, I am afraid I cannot be expected to remember any specific coal shed or its relationship to any given house after such a long period.
Sam Bloggs

From the Acting Head Postmaster:
You will no doubt be sorry to hear that the Postmaster is, at present, suffering from a nervous breakdown. Meanwhile, I am acting on his behalf.
I have before me a letter from Mrs Smith of 12 High Road in which she states she has discovered in her coal shed, buried under 5 cwt of coal, a parcel dated 17th December. As you were the delivery officer in that area at that time, would you let me have a statement please? …

BUT …

There'll always be a postman to bring your letters round.
He gets a smile of welcome, he's the greatest man in town!

THE ROYAL MAIL ARE ALWAYS VERY BUSY AT CHRISTMAS
…
BUT HOW ABOUT THIS RECOLLECTION OF
THE 12 DAYS OF CHRISTMAS?

14th December
My Dearest Darling John,
I went to the door today and the postman delivered a partridge in a pear tree. What a delightful romantic gift. Thank you, darling, for a wonderful thought. With deep love and affection always,
Your ever-loving Agnes.

15th December
My Dearest John,
Today the postman brought your very sweet gift, two turtle doves. I

am delighted, they are adorable. All my love,
Your ever-loving Agnes.

16th December
Dearest John,
Oh! How extravagant you are. I really must protest. I don't deserve
such generosity. Three French hens! I must insist you are too kind.
Your loving Agnes.

17th December
Dear John,
What can I say? Four beautiful calling birds arrived with the postman
this morning. Your kindness is really too much.
Love Agnes.

18th December
My Dearest John,
What a surprise! Today the postman delivered five golden rings – one
for each finger. You really are an impossible boy, but I love you.
Frankly all these birds are beginning to squawk and get on my nerves.
Your ever-loving Agnes.

19th December
Dear John,
When I opened the door this morning, there were actually six bloody
great geese laying eggs all over the front step! So, we are back to birds
again, are we? Where on earth do you think I can keep them all? The
neighbours are beginning to smell them and I can't sleep at night.
Please stop.
Cordially yours,
Agnes.

20th December.
John,
What is it with you and these sodding birds? Now I get seven swans-a-
swimming. Is that some sort of goddamned joke, or what? The house is
full of bird droppings, and the racket … I'm beginning to become a

nervous wreck. So, it's not funny anymore – so stop sending me any bloody birds.
Yours Agnes.

21st December
OK Buster.
I think I prefer the birds. What the hell am I going to do with eight maids-a-milking? It's not enough with all those birds – now I have eight cows dropping pancakes all over the house and they're mooing all night. Lay off.
Agnes.

22nd December
Look you.
What are you – some kind of nut? Now I have nine pipers playing – and Christ! – do they play? When they're not playing those pipes, they're chasing the milking maids through all the cow pancakes. The cows keep mooing as they are not being milked and are treading all over the birds, and the neighbours are threatening to have me evicted.
You'll get yours – Agnes.

23rd December
You rotten swine.
Now I have ten ladies dancing. How on earth anyone can call these 'whores' ladies is beyond me. They're balling the pipers all night long, the cows can't sleep and have diarrhoea, my living room is a river of shit and the landlords have just declared the building unfit for human habitation. Piss off – Agnes.

24th December
Listen you! What with eleven lords-a-leaping all over the maids and me, we shall never walk again. The pipers are fighting the lords for the crumpet and are committing sodomy with the cows. All the birds are dead and rotting, as they have been trampled on by the cows during the orgy – but not before they'd eaten my gold rings. I hope you're satisfied. Your sworn enemy. Agnes.

25th December

You stinking lousy whatever. Twelve drummers drumming have teamed up with the pipers making one hell of a bleeding din. Both lots have been buggering the Lords as well as the cows, and Christ knows what has happened to the milk maids – they've probably drowned in all the crap by now. The only way I've saved myself is by hiding up that sodding pear tree which has been so well fertilized that it's grown through the roof. I send you seasonal greetings – BALLS!
Agnes.

-7-
And While in Space

BUT ON A LIGHTER NOTE ....

Dear Earthling

Hi, I am a creature from outer space. I have transformed myself into this piece of paper. Right now, I am having sex with your fingers. I know you're enjoying it because you're smiling. Please pass me on to someone else because I'm so horny.

Thank you.

AND WHILE IN SPACE ...

The NASA Moon Problem – Instructions

You are a member of a space crew originally scheduled to rendezvous with a mothership on the lighted surface of the moon. Due to mechanical difficulties, however, your ship was forced to land at a spot some 200 miles from the rendezvous point. During landing much of the equipment aboard was damaged and, since survival depends upon reaching the mothership, the most critical items available must be chosen for the 200-mile trip. Below are listed the 15 items left intact and undamaged after landing. Your task is to rank order them in terms of their importance for your crew in allowing them to reach their rendezvous point. Place the number 1 by the most important item, and number 2 by the second most important item and so on, through to number 15 being the least important ...

Box of matches

Food concentrate

50 foot of nylon rope

Parachute silk

Portable heating unit

Two 0.45 calibre pistols and ammunition

One case dehydrated pet milk

Two 100 lb tanks oxygen

Steller map (on the moon's constellation)

Inflatable life raft

Magnetic compass

5 gallons water

Signal flares

First aid kit containing injection needles

Solar-powered FM receiver/transmitter

BACK IN THE SIXTIES THIS WAS A FAVOURITE PLOY ...

Who do you know?

Name	Colour	Occupation

Joe Louis

Christine Keeler

Ella Fitzgerald

Al Capone

Joe Montine

Kray Twins

Cassius Clay

Most people get 6 out of seven, and you say to them:
"How come you know all the gangsters, prostitutes and niggers …
but you don't know Joe Mantini? …

"He's the Pope, you ignorant Protestant!"

BACK TO THE GOOD OLD POST OFFICE …

In my time we had two cartoon characters: Stamp Bug, who promoted
stamp collecting – and Poco the elephant. His name came from the
word postcode – and he had a knot in his trunk, so that he always
remembered to use the postcode. We even had a Poco Fan Club of over
10,000 members and mailed POCO comics twice a year. There was also
a mechanical elephant that gave rides at shows. Children would sit on
his howdah, over the engine, and there were wheels hidden under each
foot. You steered him by the trunk, the accelerator was under his trunk,
and the brake behind his ear. But at one such show we had problems …

EPITAPH FOR POCO
POCO, at the Suffolk Show,
Ground his gears a little louder,
For hours he'd trundled back and forth
With kids upon his howdah.
Plodding on between the stands,
Relentlessly he travelled
Over grass, quite overgrown,
And footpaths, rudely gravelled.
No words of thanks had he received,

No kind appreciation,
Just a turbaned postman by his side
Engaged in navigation.
For two more days this scene went on
In brilliant scorching weather,
Until, at last, he'd had enough,
And reached the end of his tether.
"Dammit!" he said, to himself of course,
"Not another step I'll take."
With an unseen twitch of his flapping ears,
He deftly applied the brakes.
The postman guide, on double rate,
Was somewhat flabbergasted.
He revved the throttle, pushed and shoved,
And stood there, cursed and blasted.
A pall of smoke began to rise
From POCO's large rear quarter,
The postman lifted up his tail,
And doused the hole with water.
This thoughtless gesture was, I fear,
Precipitously hasty.
POCO's ears began to flap,
His complexion turned quite pasty.
The power behind the waterfall,
Delivered with motivation,
Flowed along the exhaust pipe
And joined the lubrication.
POCO's engine groaned and strained
And jerked with piston judder,
The kids were tossed from side to side
As the legs began to shudder.
With trunk aloft and flashing eyes
And gasps like someone dying,
The con-rod snapped the crank in two
And sent the spark plug flying.
Hysterically, the postman watched,
And reported in mumbo-jumbo,

To the PRO, "Oh, Sahib," he said,
"I've killed your bloody Dumbo!"

Earlier we mentioned Stamp Bug. One year we did everything we could to promote him. For prizes in a competition, we were going to buy mugs, but … as someone suggested they might be called Bugger Mugs, the idea was dropped. However, we had an inflatable Stamp Bug which was flown above the tent. Flown being the operative word …

THE STAMP BUG BALLOON ROBBERY

They seek him here, they seek him there,
The crime-squad seek him everywhere,
They hope to find him very soon,
The bloke who stole our big balloon.
He 'whipped' it from a place called Thame,
A town in Oxon, now in shame,
Known, in future, as a den of vice,
A showground pincher's paradise.
Thirty feet wide and fifty tall,
It's not as if the thing was small,
A swaying black and rotund publicist
The thief could be an entomologist.
One theory is an innocent dope,
Entangled himself in the anchor rope,
And yanked aloft in fear and pain,
Will be found alive in France or Spain.
Another rumour, which some disclaim,
Is the Labour Party is to blame.
Imagine Kinnock's great elation,
If he could solve the problem of inflation.
Others claim it's all a con
And the pro is having us on.
With Stamp Bug interest on the wane,
Has he pulled this stunt to prolong the reign?

WHAT ABOUT THIS FINANCIAL INSTRUCTION FOR POST OFFICE CATERING ESTABLISHMENTS?

To Finance Division:

Thank you for your letter of 26th January and the enclosure which reveals a highly developed talent for producing a surfeit of that soft, warm effluence of bureaucratic zeal which has enhanced the international reputation of Her Majesty's Postal Service.

An instance of such zeal is Mr Holdall's finely tuned conceptualisation of contextual confusion in financial terms inherent in his memorandum regarding financial arrangements for Post Office catering establishments, but he fails to hide his rampant plagiarising of early 18th century literature in the lengthy title of his ambitious piece of writing.

Brevity is not one of his strong suits, either. His writing bears the hallmark of a standard lower (rank amateurism) than that commensurate with skilled senior salaried staff and Postal Service personnel whose main aim is ambiguity of a high order (ambiguity of the highest order is reserved for Cabinet Ministers and Directors of the Post Office Board, which makes it remarkably difficult for public school crawlers to fulfil any promise of brilliant careers) such that ambiguously wise may relate the ambiguity to a total throughput cumulatively expressed, not in that sense common to those members of the public who may solve the maze, but to Harry Cott-Beeny's brilliant analysis published in Fibs Intimate No 7. We have to be careful in these matters.

Because of Holdall's quasi-innocuous fumblings and his failure to obviate the obvious, we are placed in that invidious position so much controversialised in the Horizontal Collaborators' Handbook (the well-thumbed and much-loved volume of public school crawlers) et hoc genes omen. This could jeopardise his career.

Regarding your tasteless quotation from Bumblebee's letter to the creative principle (more on this later) of Coton House, unlike your good self and the majority of your section, I am not insensible to the fact that all expenditure should lie where it falls. Indeed, most things usually do lie where they fall, especially when they are insensible, or alcoholically anaesthetised through abuse of the hospitality cabinet (need I reveal more of your department's little peccadilloes – the recent episode with Mrs Wots-er-name, which was quite unpardonable, is a blatant example).

You must appreciate that hush money can no longer be laundered through the Catering line in the Accounts Book because Eastern Region, that hotbed of infective socialist realism, if they want to know the truth, are now going through their budget every five minutes of the day with a fine tooth comb (or should I say a nit comb in your case, Rupert) to discover why an overspend is constantly recorded against them. It is common knowledge that Eastern Region are always on target with their budget, but we have had to arrange things differently. Anyway, I would suggest that Incidental Payments might be able to absorb it. But be careful here. The Managerial hyenas are drooling with ravenous appetite and with barking laughs are about to set the auditors sniffing, like Wodwo the snooping beast. The rapidly increasing figure for Incidental Payments is giving cause for concern and I am not sure where the extra costs arise but, no doubt, I shall be involved before long – especially as the Chief Cashier's secretary, Helen (is this the face that launched a thousand crates of Pedigree Bum Chum) is making noises. She seems to be putting on a lot of weight recently.

The question is – have I made myself too clear? If I have, it could prejudice the outcome of the natural progression of careerist prospects that are nurtured by the hopeful in expectation of the opportunist climate soon developing in the major re-shuffle following the rapid, untimely voluntary resignations-cum-early retirements of certain senior personnel. (What a shame to lose the Chief Auditor from the scheme of things!)

However, do not be under any illusions about pulling a fast one on me!

I've got enough evidence on your deviant activities to stop your promotion to the next grade dead in its tracks. Who was it who took a kick-back for a brakeful of mailbags allegedly lost in transit to the new office at Milton Keynes? Not so long ago, was it, eh? I believe they ended up in the Bradford area during the recent shortage for a small consideration.

Well, Rupert, I hope the above outline on financial arrangements will prove useful. As I have more important things to square, I shall have to delegate these papers to Miss Lardy (a soft touch but difficult to melt) who should be able to render a less explicit account.

P. PODD Director Finance
Universal Postal Region – 'Where The Actions Are At'
- 133 –

THIS MIGHT BE EASIER ON THE BRAIN …

Who Reads the *Daily Press*?
The Times is read by the people who run the country.
The Daily Mirror is read by the people who think they run the country.
The Guardian is read by the people who think they ought to run the country.
The Independent is read by the people who think the country ought to be run by them and people from another country.
The Daily Mail is read by the wives of the people who run the country.
The Financial Times is read by the people who own the country.
The Daily Express is read by the people who think the country ought to be run as it used to be run.
The Daily Telegraph is read by the people who think it still is.
The Sun readers don't care who runs the country …

PROVIDED SHE'S GOT BIG TITS!

ODE TO A GIRL ON HER 30th BIRTHDAY

A girl called ******* joined us one day,
To work on a charity without any pay.
A princess she was to the U's,
She started with us reading the news.
Sweet teenager and working at W&Gs
At the perfume counter she smiled and said: "Yes, please."
An era later with husband and daughter,
She's still with us and now gets even naughtier.
Her book reviews are far and wide,
Her jokes make you laugh and break your sides.
Local and lovely, a good broadcaster she,
As Deputy Programme Controller she's good to me.
Last Monday was her birthday – she's now just thirty,
Let me take off my disguise (Postman Pat) and let's be DIRTY!

-8-
Making a Telephone Call

HOW DO YOU FIND TELEPHONE CALLS?
DO YOU SOMETIMES GET THE WRONG NUMBER?

Let's look at an International call problem …

In France they have just installed a telephone line. It's a special service in Paris for the 'worried' of St Tropez, or 'overdue' of Nice, or indeed the 'jilted', 'kinky', or 'abandoned with-child' of anywhere in Europe or UK, so that calls can be made to discuss sex problems with a panel of doctors, psychiatrists, family planning experts, etc.

There is a similar system in England for the 'desperate' of Chelmsford, or the 'frantic' of Harrogate, where a number can simply be dialled and a voice will tell you the latest time, weather or test scores. This is how a country deals with its problems.

What is rather odd, though, is that the Paris service operates only from 9am to 6pm Monday to Friday. So, it is unthinkable that anyone would have a sex problem at night or during the weekend!

Perhaps in France it has become a little communistic – sex can only be practised during recognised trade union hours.

No doubt a man who, while sneaking a bit of crafty time and a half on a Saturday morning, or doing some extra-marital moonlighting when his wife thought he was at the local football, and encountering a sexual dilemma, reaching for the phone would merely get a recorded announcement asking him to hang up and ring back after 9am Monday morning when the psychiatrist clocked on duty.

Interesting, though, how this service or French connection underlines what everyone believes to be that country's obsession with sex, just as our own telephone services reflect Britain's pre-occupation with weather, time, and test match scores. None of these services are interchangeable, as the French are little interested in Britain's favourite topics.

But it seems likely that 'Dial an Expert' services are becoming very popular on the continent. In fact, in Paris there is a Gardening service too, as my friend recently found out when he needed some quick advice on his vegetable garden during his day off …

"Hello. Is that the, you know – what's it called – sort of advice service?"

"Oui, m'sieur, a votre service."

"Oh, frog are you? Funny, I was expecting someone like Percy Thrower used to be. Still, never mind. Look, what it's about … well, actually I wanted to talk to someone about the size of my cucumber, know what I mean – cucumber?"

"Oui, m'sieur, je comprends. It does not matter what euphemism you care to give it. Speak freely."

"Eh? Oh, right-ho. Well, it's like this … last year, mine was the biggest cucumber for miles around. I had the tiniest King Edward's you ever saw, but my cucumber was a whopper. Well, I'll tell you – I showed it to the vicar's wife one day, and she was flabbergasted. She said it was two inches thicker than the vicars and he'd been expecting to win a prize with his …"

"M'sieur, please one moment. I do not understand. You mean zat en Angleterre ze men show zair, er, cucumbers to ze clergymen's wifes?"

"Certainly. Show 'em to anyone, don't we? How else can we find out who's got the biggest?"

"And zis is important to you to 'ave ze big er cucumber. Tres

extradordinaire. 'Ow do you compare zem?"

"Well, we all go down to the village fete and slap our cucumbers on the table. Someone comes along and measures them – and the bloke with the biggest wins the cup."

"Mon Dieu!"

"So anyway, like I said, last year mine was the biggest in the county. Won prizes everywhere it did. But this year, I dunno – maybe it's the cold weather, but it's such a titchy little one – I'm ashamed to show it to anyone. They'd all laugh."

"You mean it's shrunk! 128ee r cucumbaire 'as shrunk!"

"No, 'course not! It's a different one, innit? I grow a new one every year, don't I? Blimey, don't you do that in France?"

"Non, m'sieur, grace a Dieu we do not. We cling to ze same, er, cucumbaire all our lifes."

"Strewth, funny bloody lot you are! Must be shrivelled up old things, hardly worth exhibiting. Anyway, what I want to know is – what shall I do about this puny one I've got? Shall I cut it off and hope a new one will grow in time or …"

"Non, m'sieur, absolument non! Do not cut anysing. I implore you. Ecountez, give me your address and I will zend an ambulance round at once …"

And so, the conversation ended with a distinguished psychiatrist and an Englishman staring gloomily into his cold frame and wondering whether some new vegetable resuscitation scheme had replaced the pay beds in the hospitals!

BASIC RULES FOR PLEASURING THE BOSS

1. Don't give nasty surprises.

2. If there's a problem above your level, talk about it in good time.

3. Never ask for an immediate decision.

4. See your job in context of the business, not just your part.

5. Don't send just the clever or smart memos, there are other ones.

6. Prepare the case before you meet.

7. To answer complex issues, don't submit a paper and talk at the same time as the boss is reading.

8. Press your views hard and, once the decision is made, carry it out … even if you don't like it.

9. Positive people offer solutions and have initiative to complete tasks successfully. Whining people say everything is impossible and are depressing. They don't improve the day.

10. Be brief – the boss has lots of other problems.

BUT CAREERS IN MANAGEMENT RESULT IN ...

Whiz kids,
Go getters,
Ulcer seeker
Rat race entrants!

APRIL FOOL …

In Post Office Public Relations, we had a fantastic idea of getting our message into the community. The purchase and conversion of a double-decker bus into an Exhibition Vehicle. Reception and display area downstairs, with video cinema, galley and VIP lounge on the top deck. Imagine my surprise at this telex … the vehicle was to be converted up North at Bamber Bridge.

URGENT:

Following a slight incident at Bamber Bridge over the Easter Weekend, I need to discuss with you urgently a revised specification for your publicity bus.

I am sending under separate cover an invoice for the work done by Bamber Bridge up to date and would appreciate prompt payment of the account. A small charge has been included on behalf of Preston Fire Service. I regard this as quite reasonable, considering the amount of foam used.

Reports from Bamber Bridge suggest that there are enough salvageable parts to convert a transit type vehicle to your original design. Please let me know when you can supply a vehicle of this type. There would be a slight surplus of special carpet, however. Alternatively, we could create a single-decker vehicle from what remains of your former ex-London Transport double-decker.

Please contact me before noon today to discuss the matter in detail.

R.M. Smart
Regional Fleet Engineer
1st April

AND ANOTHER YEAR …

After a train journey a few weeks earlier with British Airways Publicity girl, this arrived from TVS in Southampton:

Dear

I propose basing a programme in my forthcoming series 'Monday's People' on Southend, which falls within our franchise area.

The idea is to find three dynamic personalities who have helped fashion the town to its present form. One of these is likely to be Mike Kay from British Air Ferries, and another could well be from the Post Office, in view of the new sorting office which I understand will soon be in operation.

I am looking for someone of character and personality who also has something informative and entertaining to say. If you are the person I met some weeks ago on a train journey to Norwich, perhaps you might yourself be available for the programme?

I regret that as I have not yet moved into my office, I shall not be available for a week or two, but I look forward to receiving your comments in due course.

Yours sincerely,

Roz Hanby

HOW ABOUT A CALCULATOR QUIZ?

A girl of 13 had a breast of 84 *(put in 84)* or was it 45 *(put in 45)*. She went to the doctor who said 0 *(put in 0)*. He said, "Take these tablets 2 times a day" *(put in 2)* but instead she took them 4 times a day *(multiply the figure by 4)*.

How did she end up?

Turn the calculator upside down …

Then there's the Miners' story ...

The miners saw the Prime Minister and asked for an increase of £135 a week, *(put in 135)*. They said the last big increase of any significance was in 1927 *(put in 1927)* and since then they had only had 4 small increases *(multiply by 4)*.

What did the Prime Minister say?

Turn your calculator upside down to find out!

Then there's the story of Post Office Counters Ltd and their recent competition to find the Best Sub Post Office in Essex. Here are some of the entries …

I nominate St. George's for the Worst Sub Post Office, because it is the most unclean, unfriendliest and disorganised.

I nominate St. George's for the Worst Sub Post Office, because he is an utterly ignorant pig!

I nominate St. George's as the Worst Sub Post Office, because he short-changes old age pensioners.

I nominate St. George's as the Worst Sub Post Office, because it is very slow service and he is impolite!

I nominate Whitmore Way as the Worst Sub Post Office, because slow service – man don't care if he serves or not despite queue.

I nominate East Leigh for the Best Sub Post Office, because life would be difficult without it.

I nominate Lexden Heath for the Best Sub Post Office, because it is
not run by the Patel family.

I nominate Lexden Heath for the Best Sub Post Office, because the
sub-postmaster has no hair!

I nominate Marks Tey for the Best Sub Post Office, because my wife
works there and, if I don't, she'll beat me up!

I nominate Southend for the Best Sub Post Office because, everyone
who works there has got a huge PENIS!

I WONDER HOW THEY KNOW?

THE BUDGET

The country was in a terrible state,
When the Commons arose for a budget debate,
It was quite a few minutes before the Chancellor spoke,
And then he said, "Sex will cost you £10 a poke".

Whether you're short, little, long, fat or thick,
The tax will be paid on the use of your dick.
Then Tony Benn said, "Now look, Chancellor dear,
Will this apply to the boys who are queer?"

Then Ted Heath arose and looked rather glum,
"Will I be exempt, 'cos I look like a bum?"
The Chancellor replied and sounded quite airy,
"The tax will be double if you act like a fairy!"

The opposition arose with tremendous applause,
And grabbed the PM and ripped off their drawers,
They straddled the aisles and rode at will,

Then shouted aloud, "Put that on my bill."

The Labour leader shouted, "I'll have to resign,
I haven't had sex for a very long time.
I dream every night of a fanny to finish,
But I get no response from my darling Glenys."

The debate carried on but, oh, what a sight!
Some started to w**k and did it all night.
The Speaker then said, "Let the voters decide,
But I think they will settle for £10 a ride."

So, now in the bedrooms of Britain at night,
There's many a fanny that's closed good and tight.
We're taxed on our booze and we're taxed on our smoking …
But we didn't expect to be taxed on our poking.

If £10 a grind is the price we must pay,
The answer is this – with ourselves we must play.
To quench our frustrations we now have to w**k,
And, for the state of the country, we've the Chancellor to thank.

But whatever party is in power, the only revenue they can obtain is by
TAX. Recently a review was made by Inland Revenue and they found
that the only thing they have not taxed is (for men) your WILLY.

This is only due to the fact that:

40% of the time it is hanging around unemployed.

30% of the time it is pissed off.

20% of the time it is hard up.

10% of the time it is employed but operates in total darkness.
(Furthermore, it has two dependants and they are both nuts!)

Accordingly, after November 1997, the willy will be taxed based on its size, using the Willy Checker Scale below.

Determine your category and insert the additional Tax under 'Other Taxes', part V, line 61.

WILLY CHECKER SCALE

10 –12 inches	Luxury Tax	£50
8 – 9 inches	Pole Tax	£25
6 – 7 inches	Privilege Tax	£15
4 – 5 inches	Nuisance Tax	£ 5

Note:
Anyone under four (4) inches is eligible for a refund. Do not apply for an extension. Males with Willies exceeding twelve (12) inches should file under Capital Gains.

Yours truly,

Robin J. Cutcherpeckeroff
HM Inspector of Taxes

Someone who may have paid too much tax on the size of his Willy, was a Mr Humphries who retired as Managing Director of his company last week. His funeral will take place at South London Crematorium on Monday. He was not available for comment today!

But, with Willies in mind, a letter was received by Mr Humphries from the BIG CONDOM COMPANY. (Perhaps he was the MD!)

69 Missionary Drive
Dickbury

HUMPSHIRE
ON69 WEGO

We regret to inform you that you have been unsuccessful with your application to model and represent our product – Big Condoms!

Although during your interview our Board of Directors found your general appearance not displeasing, our female Promotions Manager and her staff felt that your wearing of our product in advertisements or otherwise, does not portray a positive romantic image for our company. A loose, baggy and wrinkled condom is not considered romantic or attractive.

We appreciate your interest and thank you for your time. We will retain your application for future consideration and, if by any chance we discover there is a market for micro-mini condoms, we will be in touch as you would no doubt be perfectly equipped to demonstrate such a product for us.

We send our greetings to your wife and/or girlfriend, and our deepest sympathy.

Once again we thank you for your interest and hope that you will remember our Company slogans:

Cover your stump before you hump …
Don't be silly, protect your Willy ...
Never deck her with an unwrapped pecker ...
Before you attack her, wrap your wacker ...
If you're not going to sack it go home and whack it!

Burley Dickin (President)

SO, A GUIDE TO SAFETY AND 'SAFE FAX' …

(Fax machines were commonly used to transmit documents before the world of emails!)

Q. Do I have to be married to have safe Fax?

A. Although married people Fax quite often, there are many single people who Fax complete strangers every day.

Q. My parents say they never had Fax when they were young and were only allowed to write memos to each other until they were 21. How old do you think someone should be before they can Fax?

A. Faxing can be performed at any age, once you have learned the correct procedures.

Q. If I Fax to myself, will I go blind?

A. Certainly not, as far as we can see.

Q. There is a place on our street where you can go and pay to Fax. Is this legal?

A. Yes, many people have no other outlet for their Fax drive, and pay a 'professional' when their needs to Fax become too great.

Q. Should a cover always be used for Faxing?

A. Unless you are really sure of the one you are Faxing, a cover should be used to ensure safe Fax.

Q. What happens when I correctly do the procedure and I Fax prematurely?

A. Don't panic! Many people prematurely Fax when they haven't Faxed for a long time. Just relax and start over. Most people won't mind if you try again.

Q. I have a personal and business Fax. Can transmissions become mixed up?

A. Being bi-Faxual can be confusing but, as long as you use a cover with each one, you won't transmit anything you're not supposed to.

So, how safe is safe Fax for MEN?

And what about MEN?

Some thoughts about the male of the species …

What is the insensitive bit at the base of the penis called?
The man.

What's the difference between Government Bonds and men?
Bonds mature!

How are men like noodles?
They're always in hot water, they lack taste, and they need dough.

Why do men like BMWs?
They can spell it.

What do a vagina, an anniversary, and a toilet have in common?
Men always miss them.

Why are men like popcorn?
They satisfy you, but only for a little while.

Why are men and spray paint alike?
One squeeze and they're all over you.

Why are men like blenders?
You need one, but you're not quite sure why.

Why is food better than men?
Because you don't have to wait an hour for seconds.

Why do so many women fake orgasm?
Because so many men fake foreplay.

Why are women so bad at mathematics?
Because men keep telling them that this <_____> is 12 inches.
Why do men like frozen microwave dinners so much?
They like being able to eat and make love in under 5 minutes.

Why would women be better off, if men treated them like cars?
At least then they would get a little extra attention every 6 months or
50,000 miles, whichever came first.

What do you call a man who expects to have sex on the second date?
Slow.

How many men does it take to screw in a light bulb?
One – men will screw anything.

Why do men have a hole in their penis?
So oxygen can get to their brains.

What is the difference between men and pigs?
Pigs don't turn into men when they drink.

What do ceramic tiles and men have in common?
If you lay them right the first time, you can walk on them for life.

What do you call a man with half a brain?
Gifted.

What is the difference between a man and a catfish?
One is a bottom-feeding scrum sucker and the other is a fish.

What did God say after creating man?
"I can do better."

Husband: "Want a quickie?"
Wife: "As opposed to what?"

Why do men want to marry virgins?
They can't stand criticism.

I went to the Country Fair. They had one of those 'Believe-It-Or-Not'
shows. They had a man born with a penis and a brain.

What do you have, when you have two little balls in your hand?
A man's undivided attention.

What are the two reasons why men don't mind their own business?
1. No mind   2. No business.

How is a man like a snowstorm?
Because you don't know when he is coming, how many inches you'll
get, or how long it'll stay.

Did you hear about the banker who's a great lover?
He knows first-hand the penalty for early withdrawal.

Why are men like laxatives?
They irritate the shit out of you.

What do you call an intelligent man in America?
A tourist.

Why do jocks play on artificial turf?
To keep them from grazing.

If men got pregnant ... abortion would be available in convenience
stores and drive-through windows.

Why do men name their penises?
Because they want to be on a first-class name basis with the person who makes all their decisions.

Why is it so hard for women to find men that are sensitive, caring, and good looking?
Because they already have boyfriends.
(Haha ... a good one!)

Did you hear about the man who won the gold medal at the Olympics?
He had it bronzed.

Why do men like masturbation?
It's sex with someone they love.

What is gross stupidity?
144 men in one room.

Husband: "I don't know why you wear a bra; you've got nothing to put in it."
Wife: "You wear briefs, don't you?"

What's the difference between a porcupine and a Corvette?
The porcupine has pricks on the outside.

How many men does it take to pop popcorn?
Three – one to hold the pan, and two others to show off and shake the stove.

What is a man's view of safe sex?
A padded headboard.

How do men sort their laundry?
'Filthy' and 'Filthy but Wearable'.

Only a man would buy a £500 car and put a £4,000 stereo in it.

Why did God create man?
Because a vibrator can't mow the lawn.

Why were men given larger brains than dogs?
So they wouldn't hump women's legs at cocktail parties.

Two guys were strolling down the street when one guy exclaimed, "How sad – a dead bird!" The other man looked up and said, "Where?"

Why does the stupid man put ice in his condom?
To keep the swelling down.

MAN LIKES TO ENJOY HIMSELF!

When the Creator was making the world, he told Man he was giving him 20 years of normal sex life. Man was unhappy about this and asked for more – but was refused.

The monkey was then offered 20 years. "I don't need 20," protested the monkey, "ten will do."

"May I have this extra ten years?" pleaded Man, and this time the Creator graciously agreed.

Then he offered the noble lion 20 years. The lion didn't want more than ten either, so Man asked for the surplus and was granted ten more years.

The donkey was offered 20 years but said ten was ample. Man again begged for the spare ten years and got them.

This perhaps explains why Man has 20 years of normal sex life, ten years of monkeying around, ten years 'lion' about it, and ten years of making an ass of himself.

-9-
Do Relationships Work

SO, DO RELATIONSHIPS WORK?

Here are 30 good reasons to be glad you don't have a boyfriend!

1. You have heaps of time to be completely selfish and think about Number 1. Your time is your own, your dosh is your own, and let no silly boy attempt to come between you and your inner-peace (man!).

2. You can concentrate on doing some serious bonding with your girl friends (without using superglue).

3. Your phone seat is saved from getting completely worn down by nightly three-hour sessions of love warblings. And you don't have to hide in the broom cupboard when the phone bill arrives.

4. You are relieved of endless emotional trauma and heartache. No rows, so no end-of-the-world sobbing, no worrying about being chucked. No "Why hasn't he phoned?" … no "Why is he being horrible to me?" etc.

5. You don't have to keep explaining that a dress is not called a skirt, nor that 'frock' is not a general term for things girls wear.

6. You can spend hours carefully applying your most vivid red lipstick, secure in the knowledge that your efforts will have maximum effect whilst remaining undisturbed all evening.

7. You don't get grief off your dad about where you've been and what you've been up to and whether that young man has been putting his hands where he shouldn't!

8. You don't have to tolerate the whiff of sweaty trainers – unless, of

course, you yourself happen to wear trainers and sweat a lot.

9. You don't get nervous around deeply attractive girls as the dark evil spectre of jealousy never gets to rear its ugly head. Well, you've got no-one to fight over, have you?

10. You don't need to steel yourself for the disappointment of a bare doormat on Valentine's Day. And you can send as many cards as you like with a free conscience!

11. One less birthday to shell out for, one less present choice to agonise over, one less Birthday Person to have to be unremittingly nice to for a whole day.

12. You can relish the joy of flirting outrageously, excluding X-factor and meeting as many meaningful gazes with your own across crowded rooms as you like without fear of retribution.

13. You don't have to go through the embarrassment of explaining the cause of your axe-wielding oversensitive neurotic-bitch-from-hell PMT moods.

14. You don't have to pretend to be the slightest bit interested in football, penalties, that useless Ref, off-side, etc.

15. You can save heaps of money on not having to bribe your younger siblings to leave you in peace for a good snog. And the little blighters have one less thing to tease you about.

16. Your lips remain un-swollen, your knees un-tremblesome, and your chin un-distressed by bristle rash from the effects of over-zealous snogging.

17. You don't have to endure the yawn-some and embarrassing "Listen young lady, it's about time we talked about the birds and the bees" chat from your mum. For the birds only tweet and the bees only buzz, as far as you're concerned.

18. Spaghetti 145olognese, chicken kiev, garlic bread … yes, you can eat as much of these as you like and no-one can grumble that you're not kissing sweet.

19. You don't have to fake gratitude and enthusiasm for hideous gifts such as pink teddies wearing t-shirts that say "I wuv U" and albums by an indie band that you've secretly detested.

20. You don't have to massage anyone's ego, understand anyone's insecurities or endure anyone's angst … except for your own, of course.

21. You get to eat your first *and* last Rolo … in fact, the entire packet, followed by a family size box of Maltesers, a big Mac and large fries. And no-one can reproach you for having a less than bird like appetite.

22. You don't have to worry about any family members getting their hands on your 'Secret Confess All Diary' unless, of course, you made the foolish mistake of confessing all about what you think of family members!

23. You don't have to put up with anyone's snotty mates, snotty mates' awful jokes and snotty mates' dreary girlfriends.

24. You can blub unashamedly at all the soppy films you like and not care in the least when your mascara runs and you start dribbling with emotions.

25. You don't have to check your neck for love-bites when you get home from a night out. Hence, you don't need to get up early the next day to apply layers of foundation and look rather foolish wearing a very ornate choker.

26. You don't have to live at the mercy of someone's crabby misunderstood moods, and you can have plenty of your own whenever you feel like it.

27. You don't have to sit and stare at that obstinate phone for hours on a Friday night, hoping it will ring.

28. You can save a fortune on breath freshener which will be surplus to requirements.

29. Your toilet seat will get left up just that little bit less often.

30. You can swoon over the stars you like without being sulked at.

BUT, NOWADAYS, THERE ARE CUSTOMS IN THE WAY YOU PROVIDE LIP SERVICE …

UNFINISHED BUSINESS – A natural successor to the detonator, this kiss leaves you in an awkward situation. Once you have succumbed to a fully-fledged passionate embrace, what do you do when you next meet? Usually you are forced to return to a bland peck on each cheek, but a knowing look between you says it all!

AFTER DINNER MINT – Having gazed into each other's eyes throughout dinner-a-deux, it would be rude not to.

THE KISS OF LIFE – Invaluable if you are drowning, mouth-to-mouth resuscitation will always save the day.

THE MEDIA KISS – You don't actually touch cheeks, but both kiss the air and go on to the next.

THE BOTCHED JOB – A favourite at parties, you both hone in for the double (one on each cheek) but go for the same cheek and end up like birds pecking the air in a courtship ritual. Or, you go for a friendly one on the cheek, he's hoping for a lip-smacker, and noses biff.

THE HAUL IN – Someone you have no desire to kiss, grabs your politely proffered hand and uses it to haul you in for a kiss.

THE CORPORATE KISS – Probably the most alarming. Colleagues who wouldn't dream of kissing you at work feel sufficiently liberated meeting you in a new context to kiss you, leaving you no choice but to co-operate.

THAT'S MY GIRL – This kiss lands on your mid-forehead or, even worse, on the top of your head. Utterly patronising, it implies you're too sweet for words.

THE DETONATOR – This is a lethal cocktail passionately concocted between two who have commitments elsewhere and know they shouldn't really kiss but just can't resist it. Packed with pent-up ardour, there's no knowing what will happen when this explodes.

AND, WITH OFFICIAL EVENTS IN MIND, HOW ABOUT THE WEARING OF TIES FOR MEN?

Ties can be worn in three different ways:

1. In the conventional manner around the neck, worn either knotted on a shirt buttoned at the collar in the winter, or tied loosely in the summer in a casual manner.

2. Around the trousers as a belt, especially so if the conventional attire fails, or as an added safety feature to complement the belt and/or braces arrangement usually worn by the wearer.

10.   In the 'Rambo' style and worn lightly knotted around the head, the wearer of this style may also wish to remove upper body clothing and adorn the torso and face with an appropriate coloured theatrical grease paint!

So, would you turn up at work with an unconventional way of wearing your tie? Would the boss be impressed or concerned?

HOW ABOUT CHECKING YOUR STARS TO SEE IF TODAY, OR ANY DAY, WOULD BE YOUR SORT OF DAY?

Aquarius (Jan 21 – Feb 19)
You have an inventive mind and are inclined to be progressive. You lie a great deal. On the other hand, you are inclined to be careless and impractical, causing you to make the same mistakes over and over again. People think you are stupid!

Pisces (Feb 20 – March 20)
 You are a spring-like person – someone who just loves tidying up, someone who is smart, but never leaves a room untidy – you are just OTT!

Aries (March 21 – April 20)
You are a sleeper, a quiet person who sleeps lots – but in groups you are a sleeper in that you don't always listen to what is going on, then you have to ask about the conversation. Hey you … try and wake up!

Taurus (April 21 – May 20)
You are practical and persistent. You have a dogged determination and work like hell. Most people think you are stubborn and bull headed. You are a communist.

Gemini (May 21 – June 20)
You are a quick and intelligent thinker. People like you because you are bisexual, however you are inclined to expect too much for too little. This means you are cheap. Gemini's are known for committing incest.

Cancer (June 21 – July 21)
You are sympathetic and understanding to other peoples' problems. They think you are a sucker. You are always putting things off. That's why you will never make anything of yourself. Most welfare recipients are Cancer people.

Leo (July 22 – Aug 21)
You consider yourself a born leader. Others think you are pushy. Most Leo people are bullies. You are vain and dislike honest criticism. Your arrogance is disgusting. Leo people are known thieves.

Virgo (Aug 22 – Sept 21)
You are the logical type and hate disorder. This nit-picking is sickening to your friends. You are cold and unemotional and sometimes fall asleep when making love. Virgos make good bus drivers.

Libra (Sept 22 – Oct 21)
You are the artistic type and have a difficult time with reality. If you are a man, you are more likely to be queer. Chances for employment and monetary gain are excellent. Most Libra women are good prostitutes. All Libras die of venereal disease.

Scorpio (Oct 22 – Nov 21)
You are shrewd in business and cannot be trusted. You shall achieve the pinnacle of success because of your total lack of ethics. Most Scorpio people are murderers.

Sagittarius (Nov 22 – Dec 21)
You are optimistic and enthusiastic. You have a reckless tendency to rely on luck since you lack talent. The majority of Sagittarians are drunks or dope fiends. People laugh at you a great deal.

Capricorn (Dec 22 – Jan 20)
You are conservative and afraid of taking risks. You don't do much of anything and are lazy. There has never been a Capricorn of any importance. Capricorns should avoid standing too long as they tend to take root and become trees.

SO WHAT ABOUT YOU … WHAT ARE YOU REALLY LIKE ?

So boy are you corny, you act like a square at the fair, a goon from Sasketu, you come on like a broken arm, you're a sad apple, a long hair, a corn husker, in other words you don't send me, so bail out brother, get lost and take your rat cat!

BUT I AM BLACK

I was born 'Black'.
When I go out in the sun, I am black.
When I am sick, I am black.
When I am dying I am black.
When they bury me, I am black.

You are 'White' …
You were born pink.
When you go out in the sun, you turn red,
Then you go brown.
When you get sick, you turn white.
When you are dying, you go grey.
When they bury you, you are purple.

And you've got the nerve to call ME coloured!

But whoever you are, in work or unemployed, there are always EDUCATION COURSES to sign up for …

Designed to heighten your awareness of the need for DEVELOPMENT, in a variety of subjects and to develop communication skills for those wanting to meet the challenge of our joining the European Community.

SELF-IMPROVEMENT COURSE

SI10   Creative Suffering
SI11   Overcoming Peace of Mind
SI12   Ego Gratification Through Violence
SI13   Overcoming Self-Doubt Through Pretence and Ostentation
SI14   Whine Your Way Through Alienation
SI15   Guilt Without Sex
SI16   Feigning Knowledge – A Career Advancement Strategy
SI17   Children – An Avoidable Distraction in Education and Decision Making
SI18   Keeping Facts Out of Your Management Structure
SI19   Carrying a Piece of Paper While Walking Briskly
SI20   Developing the Primal Shrug

BUSINESS AND CAREER COURSES

BC10   Money – It Can Make You Rich
BC11   Packaging, Marketing and Selling Your Child
BC12   Career Opportunities in Bingham
BC13   How to Profit from Your Own Body
BC14   The Under-Achiever's Guide to Very Small Business Opportunities
BC15   Supply Teaching in the Orkneys
BC16   Tattooing Your Colleagues as an Income Supplement
BC17   Credit Purchasing with Your Kidney Donor Card

FITNESS & HEALTH

FH10   The Joys of Hyprochondria
FH11   High-Fibre Sex
FH12   Create Tooth Decay
FH13   Skate Your Way to Regularity
FH14   Understanding Nudity
FH15   Obesity and Trampolining

FH16   The Repair and Maintenance of Your Virginity
FH17   Optional Body Functions
FH18   Tap Dance Your Way to Social Ridicule
FH19   Exercise and Acne
FH20   Baked Beans and the Contortionist

CRAFT COURSES

C10   Bonsai Your Pet
C11   Self-Actualisation Through Macrame
C12   Needlecraft for Junkies
C13   Drawing Genitalia in Soft Pastel Shades (Spring Term only)
C14   Artistic Chicken Trussing for Vegetarians
C15   Orchestrated Flatulence Appreciation
C16   Breaking and Entering Department Lockers

HOME ECONOMICS COURSES

HE10   Cultivating Viruses in Household Refrigerators
HE11   Sinus Drainage in the Modern Marriage
HE12   Basic Kitchen Taxidermy (i.e. Stuffed Prawn Curry)
HE13   Khmer Rouge Cookery for Beginners
HE14   How to Convert a Wheelchair into a Dune Buggy
HE15   How to Convert Your Citroen 2CV into a Porsche Turbo

But with LOVE all things are possible!

This message is sent to you for good luck. The original is in NEWLAND. It has been sent around the world nine times. The luck has now been sent to you. You will receive good luck within four days of reading this – provided, in return, you copy it out and send it on.

This is no joke. You will receive good luck in the mail. Send no money. Send copies to people that you think need good luck. Do not send money, as fate has no price. Do not keep a copy of this message. It must leave your hands within 96 hours.

An RAF officer received £47,000. While abroad, Gene Welch lost his wife, 51 days after receiving the letter – he had failed to circulate the letter. Before her death he received £7M after circulating the letter just prior to her death.

Please send 20 copies and see what happens in four days!

The chain letter originated in Venezuela, and was written by Soul Anthony De Group, a missionary from South Africa. Since the copy must tour the world, you must make 20 copies and send them to friends and associates. After a few days you will get a surprise. This is true, even if you are not superstitious.

Do note the following: Constantine Dine received the chain in 1985. He asked his secretary to make 20 copies and send them out. A few days later he won the lottery of over 20 million dollars. Carlo Daddit, an office employee, received the letter and forgot it had to leave his hands within 96 hours. He lost his job. Later, after finding the letter again, he got a better job and he mailed out 20 copies. A few days later he got an even better job. Dalan Fairchild received the letter and, not believing, he threw the letter away. Nine days later he died.

In 1967 this letter was received by a young woman in California. It was very faded and barely visible. She promised herself that she would re-type the letter and sent it on. But she put it aside to do it later and she forgot. She was plagued with various problems, including expensive car repairs. The letter did not leave her hands in 96 hours. She finally typed the letter as promised, and within days she won a brand new automobile!

Remember – send no money and do not sign.

THROUGHOUT THE WORLD THERE ARE NOTICES AND SIGNS.

Here are some samples …

In a Beijing hotel:
Is forbidden to steal hotel towels please. If you are not a person to do such a thing is please not to read notise.

In a Bucharest hotel lobby:
The lift is being fixed for the next day. During that time we regret that you will be unberarable.

In a Leipzig elevator:
Do not enter lift backwards, and only when lit up.

In a Belgrade hotel elevator:
To move the cabin, push button for wishing floor. If the cabin should enter more persons, each one should press a number of wishing floor. Driving is then going alphabetically by national order.

In a Yugoslavian hotel:
The flattening of underwear with pleasure is the job of the chambermaid.

In a Japanese hotel:
You are invited to take advantage of the chambermaid.

In a Paris hotel:
Please leave your values at the front desk.

In a hotel in Athens:
Visitors are expected to complain at the office between the hours of 9 and 11am daily.

In an advertisement by a Hong Kong dentist:
Teeth extracted by the latest Methodists.

In the lobby of a Moscow hotel across from Russian Orthodox
Monastery:
You are welcome to visit the cemetery where famous Russian and
Soviet composers, artists, and writers are buried daily except
Thursday.

In an Austrian hotel catering to skiers:
Not to perambulate the corridors during the hours of repose in the
boots of ascension.

On the Menu of a Swiss restaurant:
Our wines leave you nothing to hope for.

On the Menu of a Polish hotel:
Salad a firms own make, limpid red beet soup with cheesy dumplings
in the form of a finger, roasted duck let loose, beef rashers beaten up
in the country people's fashion.

Outside a Paris dress shop:
Dresses for street walking.

In a Rhodes tailor shop:
Oder your summers suit. Because is big rush we will execute
customers in strict rotation.

From the Soviet Weekly:
There will be a Moscow Exhibition of Arts by 150,000 Soviet
Republic painters and sculptors. These were executed over the past 2
years.

A sign posted in Germany's Black Forest:
It is strictly forbidden on our black forest camping site that people of
different sex, for instance men and women, live together in one tent
unless they are married with each other for that purpose!

THE ROYAL MAIL STORY …

Once upon a time, Royal Mail and the Japanese decide to have a competitive boat race on the River Thames. Both teams practiced long and hard to reach their peak performance. On the big day, they were as ready as they could be. The Japanese won by a mile.

After that, the Royal Mail became very discouraged by the loss and morale sagged. Senior Management decided that the reason for the crushing defeat had to be found, and a project team was set up to investigate the problem and recommend appropriate action.

Their conclusion: The problem was that the Japanese team had eight people rowing and one person steering. The Royal Mail team had one person rowing and eight people steering.

Senior Management immediately hired a consultancy company to do a study of the team's structure. Millions of pounds and several months later, they concluded that too many people were steering and not enough rowing.

To prevent losing to the Japanese next year, the team structure was changed to four Steering Managers, three Senior Managers and one Executive Steering Manager. A performance and appraisal system was set up to give the person rowing the boat more incentive to work harder and become a key performer.

"We must give him empowerment and enrichment. That ought to do it."

The next year the Japanese won by two miles. Royal Mail laid off the rower for poor performance, sold off all the paddles, cancelled all capital investment for new equipment, halted development of a new canoe, awarded high performance awards to the consultants and distributed the money saved to Senior Management!

POSTMAN JACK, POSTMAN JACK, POSTMAN JACK AND THE BEANSTALK!

In the post, Jack, a postman from darkest Buckinghamshire received a bonus package for hard work. His wife found it on the doormat and went down to Safeway, Sainsbury and Tesco to do the shopping, but they would not let her pay with a packet of seeds, no matter whose bonus it was.

On arriving home, a row ensued, and his angry wife threw the seeds out of the window. Next morning, when going to work, Jack saw a beanstalk was growing out of his garden so he thought he would blow work and climb to the top.

After two hours of climbing, he came through the clouds to see a large house. The plaque on the door read Managing Director of Royal Mail. Jack snuck in the open door, as you would, and spied a large table with a pile of gold coins on it, a solid gold book called 'How to Swindle Employees', and a pile of £10 notes.

Just then a Rolls Royce pulled up and the Managing Director got out. "Fee-fi-fo-fum, I smell the blood of a poor postman!" said a voice.

Jack, not wanting to hang around, grabbed hold of the book, some gold coins and a few notes and stuffed them into his delivery pouch. He jumped off the table and ran, pursued by the wicked Managing Director. Pausing at the beanstalk he threw the pouch down, turned and faced his chaser, gave him a V-sign and beat a hasty retreat.

When he was at the bottom, he cut the beanstalk down and shouted to his wife to come outside where he recounted his tale. On opening the pouch, they found to their disbelief that the book had turned into worthless gift vouchers, the bank notes were 20 First Class stamps, and the gold coins were a packet of seeds.

Perhaps you know of a similar tale where employees are treated like fairy tale characters? Until we meet again ...

JACKANORY!

IN AN ESSEX POST OFFICE …

A sub-postmaster stood at the pearly gates,
His face was worn and old,
He stood before the man of God,
For admission to the fold.

"What have you done," St. Peter asked,
"To gain admission here?"
"I've been a sub-postmaster
For many a long, long year."

The pearly gates swung open wide,
St. Peter rang the bell.
"Come in,' he said, "and choose your harp …
You've had your share of HELL!"

BUILDING IMPROVEMENTS …

In the early 1990s, a man called Fred West had killed, over a period of
time, a number of young women and hidden them in his house. A new
company was launched shortly afterwards …

If you want the best, try West Home Improvements.
Make no bones about it, we put body and soul into every job.
Don't have grave doubts – most of Fred's family have been into
patios, bathrooms, fireplaces, etc for years.
Wife and kids under your feet? Why not try a West special extension!
We knock the competition dead.
Skeleton staff on at weekends.
Call and see us – we guarantee you won't go elsewhere.
Contact: West Home Improvements, 25 Cromwell St, Gloucester.

NOW TO TOUCH ON RELIGION …

The new priest was so nervous at his first mass, he could hardly speak. Before his second appearance in the pulpit he asked the Monsignor how he could relax. The Monsignor said, "Next Sunday, it may help if you put some vodka in the water pitcher. After a few sips everything should go smoothly."

The next Sunday, the new priest put the suggestion into practice and was able to talk up a storm. He felt great. However, upon returning to the Rectory, he found a note from the Monsignor:

1. Next time sip rather than gulp.

2. There are 10 commandments not 12.

3. There are 12 disciples not 10.

4. We do not refer to the Cross as the 'Big T'.

5. The recommended Grace before meals is not:
"Rub-a-dub-dub, thanks for the grub, yeah, God!"

6. Do not refer to our Saviour Jesus Christ and his Apostles as:
"JC and the Boys".

7. David slew Goliath, he did not kick the shit out of him.

8. The Father, Son and Holy Ghost are never referred to as
"Big Daddy, Junior and the Spook".

9. It is always the Virgin Mary, not Mary with the cherry.

10. Last, but not least, next Wednesday there will be a Taffy-Pulling contest at St. Peters, not a Peter-Pulling contest at St. Taffys.

THE BEER PRAYER

Our lager,
Which art in barrels,
Hallowed be thy drink.
Thy will be drunk,
(I will be drunk),
At home as in the tavern.
Give us this day our foamy head,
And forgive us our spillages,
As we forgive those who spill against us.
And lead us not to incarceration,
But deliver us from hangovers,
For thine is the beer,
The bitter and the lager.
Forever and ever,
Barmen!

-10-
Is It True?

IS IT TRUE?

One day while walking around town, a Human Resources Manager was hit by a bus and was tragically killed. Her soul arrived up in Heaven, where she was met at the Pearly Gates by St. Peter himself.

"Welcome to Heaven," said St. Peter. "Before you get settled in, though, it seems we have a problem. You see, strangely enough, we've never once had an HR Manager make it this far and we're not really sure what to do with you."

"No problem, just let me in," said the woman.

"Well, I'd like to, but I have higher orders. What we're going to do is let you have a day in Hell and a day in Heaven – and then you can choose whichever one you want to spend an eternity in," the Saint replied.

"Actually, I think I've made up my mind ... I prefer to stay in Heaven," said the woman.

"Sorry, we have rules," said St. Peter ... and, with that, he put the woman in an elevator and it went down, down, down, down, down into Hell.

The doors opened and the HR Manager found herself stepping out onto the putting green of a beautiful golf course. In the distance was a country club and, standing in front of her, were all her friends – fellow HR professionals that she had worked with. They were all dressed in evening gowns and cheering for her. They ran up and kissed her on both cheeks and they talked about old times. They played an excellent round of golf and, at night, went to the country club and enjoyed an excellent steak and lobster dinner.

The HR Manager met the Devil, who was actually a really nice guy (kinda cute!) and she had a great time telling jokes and dancing. The HR Manager was having such a good time that, before she knew it, it was time to leave. Everyone shook her hand and waved goodbye as she got on the elevator.

The elevator went up, up, up, up, up, up, up and the doors opened back at the Pearly Gates and she found St. Peter waiting for her.

"Now it's time to spend a day in Heaven," he said. So the HR Manager spent the next 24 hours lounging around on the clouds and playing the harp and singing. She had a great time and, before she knew it, her 24 hours were up and St. Peter came and got her.

"So, you've spent a day in Hell and a day in Heaven – now you must choose your eternity," he said. The HR Manager paused for a second and then replied …

"Well, I never thought I'd say this – I mean – Heaven has been really great and all, but I had a better time in Hell."

So, St. Peter escorted her to the elevator and once more the HR Manager went down, down, down, down, down, back to Hell.

When the doors of the elevator opened, she found herself standing in a desolate wasteland covered in garbage and filth. She saw her friends all dressed in rags, picking up the garbage and putting it into sacks for the evening meal.

The Devil came up to her and put his arms around her and laughed at her.

"I don't understand," stammered the HR Manager. "Yesterday I was here and there was a golf course and a country club and we ate lobster and we danced and had a great time. Now all there is, is a wasteland of garbage and all my friends look miserable.

The Devil looked at her and grinned, "That's because yesterday we were recruiting you, but today you are staff."

WHY WORRY?
(Irish Philosophy)

There are only two things in life to worry about …
Either you are well, or you are sick.

If you are well –
Then there is nothing to worry about.

But, if you are sick – there are two things to worry about …
Either you will get better, or you will die.

If you get better –
Then there is nothing to worry about.

But, if you die – there are two things to worry about …
Either you will go to heaven, or you will go to hell.

If you go to heaven –
Then there is nothing to worry about.

But, if you go to hell –
You'll be so bloomin' busy shaking hands with all your old friends …
You won't have time to worry!

So … Why Worry?

SO TAKE HOLD OF EVERY MOMENT!

A friend of mine opened his wife's underwear drawer and picked up a silk-paper wrapped package.

"This," he said, "isn't any ordinary package." He unwrapped the box and stared at both the silk-paper and the box.

"She got this the first time we went to New York, 8 or 9 years ago. She has never put it on. Was saving it for a special occasion. Well, I guess this is it."

He got near the bed and placed the gift box next to the other clothing items he was taking to the undertakers; his wife had just died.

He turned and said, "Never save something for a special occasion. Every day in your life is a special occasion."

Those words changed my life. Now I read more and clean less.

I sit on the porch without worrying about anything. I spend more time with my family and less at work. I understood that life should be a source of experience to be lived up to, not survived through. I use crystal glasses every day. I'll wear new clothes to go to the supermarket, if I feel like it. I don't save my special perfume for special occasions. I use it whenever I want to.

The words 'Someday' and 'One Day' are fading away from my dictionary. If it's worth seeing, listening to or doing, I want to see, listen to, or do it now. I don't know what my friend's wife would have done if she knew she wouldn't be there the next morning; this nobody can tell. I think she might have called her relatives and closest friends. She might call old friends to make peace over past quarrels. I'd like to think she would go out for Chinese, her favourite food. It's these small things that I would regret not doing, if I knew my time had come.

I would regret it, because I would no longer see the friends I would love to meet, letters… letters that I wanted to write, 'one of these days'. I would regret and feel sad because I didn't say to my brother and sons, not enough times at least, how much I love them. Now I try not to delay, postpone or keep anything that could bring laughter and joy into our lives.

And on each morning, I say to myself that this could be a special day. Each day, each hour, each minute is special. If you got this, it's because someone cares for you and because probably there's someone you care about. If you're too busy to give this out to other people and you say to yourself that you will send it … 'one of these days' … remember that 'one day' is far away … or might never come …

This TANTRA is Indian. No matter if you are superstitious or not, spending some time reading it holds a useful message for the soul.

Here's the fun of life if you share it with others …

0 – 4 people	your life improves slightly
5 – 9 people	your life improves according to your expectations
9 – 14 people	you'll have at least 5 surprises in the next 3 weeks
15 or more people	your life improves drastically and your dreams start to take shape!

A COMMUTER'S MEMO PAD

Eat garlic bread for breakfast
Hide girlie mag inside your daily newspaper
Practice swash-buckling with brolly
Jostle for position in station, bus, tram or train
Don't let people off before you get on
Turn earphone up to max

Pretend to read newspaper
Read someone else's newspaper
Ignore the elderly and pregnant
Practice the use of the briefcase as a deadly weapon
Sleep past your stop!

A DOG NAMED SEX

Everybody who has a dog calls him 'Rover' or 'Boy'. I call mine 'Sex' as he's a great pal – but he has caused me a great deal of embarrassment. When I went to renew his dog licence, I told the man I need a licence for 'Sex'. He said he'd like one too. But I said, "This is for a dog." He said he did not care what she looked like. I said, "You don't understand, I've had 'Sex' since I was 9 years old." He winked and said, "You must have been quite a kid!"

When I got married and went on my honeymoon, I took the dog with me. I told the Hotel Clerk I wanted a room for my wife and me and a special room for Sex.

He said, "You don't need a special room; as long as you pay your bill we don't care what you do."

I said, "Look you don't seem to understand … Sex keeps me awake at night."

The clerk said, "Funny, I have the same problem."

One day I entered Sex in a contest but, before the competition began, my dog ran away. Another contestant asked me why I looked disappointed, so I told him I had planned to have Sex in the contest.

He told me I should have sold my own tickets – but I said I had hoped to win and have Sex on tv.

When my wife and I separated, we had to fight in the courts for custody of the dog. I said to the judge "Your honour, I had Sex before I was married."

The judge said the courtroom was not for confessions. Sex ran off yet again and I spent hours around town looking for him.

A policeman came up to me and asked what I was doing in the alley in town at 4am – I told him I was looking for Sex – my case is up before the judge later this week!

CONDOMS

The local political party has chosen the condom as its official emblem:

It stands for inflation.

Halts production.

Gives protection to a bunch of pricks.

And gives one a false sense of security whilst being stuffed!

AFFAIRS …

The First Affair

A married man was having an affair with his secretary. One day they went to her place and made love all afternoon. Exhausted, they fell asleep and woke at 8pm. The man hurriedly dressed and told his lover to take his shoes outside and rub them in the grass and dirt.

He put on his shoes and drove home. "Where have you been?" his wife demanded.

"I can't lie to you," he replied, "I'm having an affair with my secretary. We had sex all afternoon."

She looked down at his shoes and said, "You lying bastard, you've been playing golf all afternoon."

The 2nd Affair

A middle-aged couple had two beautiful daughters, but always talked about having a son. They decided to try one last time for the son they had always wanted. The wife got pregnant and delivered a healthy baby boy. The joyful father rushed to the nursery to see his new son. He was horrified at the ugliest child he had ever seen. He told his wife, "There's no way I can be the father of this baby. Look at the two beautiful daughters I fathered! Have you been fooling around behind my back?"

The wife smiled sweetly and replied … "Not this time!"

The 3rd Affair

A mortician was working late one night. He examined the body of Mr Schwartz, who was about to be cremated, and made a startling discovery. Schwartz had the largest private part he had ever seen!

"I'm sorry, Mr Schwartz," the mortician commented, "I can't allow you to be cremated with such an impressive private part. It must be saved for posterity." So, he removed it, stuffed it into his holdall, and took it home.

"I have something to show you – you won't believe it!" he said to his wife, opening his holdall!

"My God!" the wife exclaimed, "Schwartz is dead!"

The 4th Affair

A woman was in bed with her lover when she heard her husband opening the front door. "Hurry," she said, "stand in the corner."

She rubbed baby oil all over him, then dusted him with talcum powder. "Don't move until I tell you," she said, "pretend you're a statue ..."

"What's this?" the husband inquired, as he entered the room.

"Oh, it's a statue," she replied, "the Smiths bought one and I liked it, so I got one for us too."

No more was said, not even when they went to bed. Around 2am the husband got up, went to the kitchen and returned with a sandwich and a beer.

"Here," he said to the statue, "have this. I stood like that for two days at the Smiths and nobody offered me a dammed thing."

The 5th Affair

A man walked into a café, went to the bar and ordered a beer.

"Certainly, Sir, that'll be a £1," said the barman.

"Just a pound!" the man exclaimed. He glanced at the menu and asked, "How much for a nice juicy steak and a bottle of wine?"

"Two pounds," said the barman.

"Just two pounds!" exclaimed the man. "Where's the guy who owns this place?"

"Upstairs with my wife," said the barman.

"What's he doing upstairs with your wife?" asked the man.

The barman replied, "The same thing I'm doing to his business down here."

The 6th Affair

Jake was dying. His wife sat at the bedside. He looked up and said weakly, "I have something I must confess."

"There's no need to," his wife replied.

"No," he insisted, "I want to die in peace. I slept with your sister, your best friend, her best friend, and your mother."

"I know," she replied. "Now just rest and let the poison work!"

BUT THE PERFECT WOMAN WOULD SAY ...

1. I'll swallow it all ... I love the taste!

2. Are you sure you've had enough to drink?

3. I'm bored ... let's shave my fanny!

4. Oh, come on, what do you say we get a good porn film, a carton of beer and have my friend over for a threesome?

5. God, if I don't get to blow you soon, I'll kill myself!

6. You're so sexy when you're drunk!

7. I know it's a lot tighter back there, but would you please try again?

8. I'd rather watch you and your mates watch sport and serve you beers!

9. Let's subscribe to the porn channels!

10. Would you like to watch me go down on my girlfriend?

11. Let's go shopping so that you can look at womens' arses.

12. I love it when you play footy on Saturday – I just wish that you had time to play on Sunday too!

13. Darling – our new neighbour's daughter is sunbathing again, come and see!

14. I've decided to stop wearing clothes around the house!

15. Do me a favour, forget the stupid Valentine's day thing and buy yourself something instead!

16. That was a great fart! Try and do another one!

17. I signed up for yoga, so that I can get my ankles behind my head for you!

HAPPY BIRTHDAY!

They say one flower can speak a thousand words, so I hope that when you woke up this morning on your birthday, you had a great big smile on your face, I hope during the day the sun will be shining on you and the birds will be chirping songs for you – I hope you were the first into the bathroom this morning and you had the top of the milk on your cornflakes and the cream in your coffee.

I hope the postman called, laden down with cards and presents for you and I hope you go through the day light of step, filled with zip, zeal and vigour.

When it comes to this evening, may you celebrate your very special day with extra special friends and extra strong cocktails, perhaps with dancing, music and song – I hope everyone laughs at all your suspect jokes, I hope you come up trumps on the one-arm bandit, your ship comes in, and your horse wins at a 100/1.

I hope your night out is really hunky-dory and hope when your night on the tiles is over, someone springs a great big nice surprise on you, which really makes your day. I hope the moon glows, the stars twinkle and you feel warm all over, and your bed is snug and cozy and all your dreams are sweet and happy ones. In short, briefly, when it comes down to it, at the end of the day, I really most sincerely hope that your birthday is quite nice!

CHRISTMAS

What do you call a group of chess masters standing in a hotel lobby arguing about who made all the best moves?

Chess nuts boasting in an open foyer!

A Christmas Story …

'Twas the night before Christmas – old Santa was pissed,
He cussed out the elves and threw down his list.
Miserable little brats, ungrateful little jerks,
I have a good mind to scrap the whole works!

I've busted my ass for damn near a year,
Instead of: "Thanks Santa!" … Oh, what do I hear?

The old lady bitches 'cause I work late at night,
The elves want more money – reindeer all fight.

Rudolph got drunk and goosed all the maids,
Donner is pregnant and Vixen has aids.
And just when I thought that things would get better,
Those assholes from the tax sent me a letter.
They say I owe taxes– if that ain't damn funny,
Who the hell ever sent Santa Claus any money?

And the kids these days – they all are the pits,
They want the impossible – those mean little shits!
I spent a whole year making wagons and sleds,
Assembling dolls – their arms, legs and heads.
I made a ton of yo-yos – no request for them …
They want computers and robots – they think I'm IBM.

Flying through the air – dodging the trees,
Falling down chimneys and skinning my knees.
I'm quitting this job, there's just no enjoyment,
I'll sit on my fat arse and draw unemployment.

There's no Christmas this year now, you know the reason …
I found me a blonde – I'm going south for the season!

ENGLAND, IRELAND & SCOTLAND

There's an Englishman, an Irishman and a Scotsman, all talking about their teenage daughters. The Englishman says, "I was cleaning my daughter's room the other day and I found a packet of cigarettes. I was really shocked as I didn't know she smokes."

The Scotsman says, "That's nothing. I was cleaning my daughter's room the other day when I came across a half-full bottle of Vodka. I was really shocked as I didn't know she drank!"

With that the Irishman says, "Both of you have nothing to worry about.

I was cleaning my daughter's room the other day, when I found a packet of condoms. I was really shocked. I didn't even know she had a willy."

STARS

Two male pop stars and a female went out for a night on the town. As they left the night-club, the female stopped and got her head stuck between the railings of the fence opposite the club. One of the male popstars decided to take full advantage of this and lifted up her little skirt, pushed her thong to one side and gave her a good seeing to.

He said to the other male pop star, "It's your turn now!", but he started crying. Asked why he was crying, he said, "My head won't fit between the railings as I have a big head!"

BAR TALK

A blind man enters a Ladies Bar by mistake. He finds his way to a bar stool and orders a drink. After sitting there for a while he yells to the bartender – "Hey, do you want to hear a blonde joke?"

The bar immediately falls absolutely quiet and, in a deep husky voice, the woman next to him says, "Before you tell that joke, sir, I think it just fair – giving that you are blind, you should know five things:

1. The bartender is a blonde girl.

2. The bouncer is a blonde girl.

3. I'm a 6 feet tall, 220 lb blonde woman, with a black belt in karate.

4. The woman sitting next to me is blonde and is a professional weight lifter.

5. The lady to your right is a blonde and is a professional wrestler.

So, do you really want to tell your joke, Mister?

LEAVING WORK EARLY!

Three girls all worked in the same office with the same female boss. Each day they noticed the boss left work early. One day the girls decided that, when the boss left, they would leave right behind her. After all, she never called or came back to work, so how would she know they went home early?

The brunette was thrilled to be home early. She did a little gardening, spent playtime with her son, and went to bed early.

The redhead was elated to be able to get in a quick workout at the spa, before meeting a dinner date.

The blonde was happy to get home early and surprise her husband but, when she got to her bedroom, she heard muffled noises from inside. Slowly and quietly she cracked open the door and was mortified to see her husband in bed with her lady boss. Gently she closed the door and crept out of her house.

The next day, at their coffee break, the brunette and redhead planned to leave early again and they asked the blonde if she was going with them?

"No way!" the blonde exclaimed. "I almost got caught yesterday."

SENIOR CITIZENS ARE THE NATIONS LEADING CARRIERS OF AIDS!

Hearing Aids, Band Aids, Roll Aids, Walking Aids, Medical Aids and, most of all, Monetary Aids to their Children.

THE GOLDEN YEARS HAVE COME AT LAST!

I cannot see, I cannot pee, I cannot chew, I cannot screw,
My memory shrinks, my hearing stinks,
No sense of smell, I look like hell,
My body's drooping, got trouble pooping.

So, the golden years have come at last?
Well … the Golden Years can kiss my ARSE!

YET WE ARE SURVIVORS

For those who were born before 1940 …

We were born before television, before penicillin, polio shots, frozen foods, Xerox, plastic, contact lenses, video, frisbees and the Pill.

We were born before radar, credit cards, split atoms, laser beams and ball-point pens, before dishwashers, tumble dryers, electric blankets, air-conditioners, drip-dry clothes … and before man walked on the moon.

We got married first and then lived together (how quaint can that be!) We thought fast food was what you ate in Lent, a 'Big Mac' was an oversized raincoat and 'crumpet' was what you had for tea.

We existed before house-husbands, computer dating, dual careers, and when a 'meaningful relationship' meant getting along with cousins and 'sheltered accommodation' was where you waited for a bus.

We were before day-care centres, group homes and disposable nappies. We never heard of FM and internet radio, tape decks, electric typewriters, artificial hearts, word processors, yoghurt, computers, iPods, iPads, hand-held telephones and young men wearing earrings.

For us time-sharing meant togetherness, a 'chip' was a piece of wood or a fried potato, 'hardware' meant nuts and bolts, 'software' wasn't a word and match fees were paid by 15-a-side rugby players, not received.

Before 1940 'Made in Japan' meant junk, the term 'making out' referred to how you did in your exams, 'stud' was something that fastened a collar to a shirt and 'going all the way' meant staying on a double-decker bus to the bus depot.

Pizzas, McDonalds and instant coffee were unheard of. In our day cigarette smoking was 'fashionable', grass was mown, 'coke' was kept in the coal house, a 'joint' was a piece of meat you had on Sundays, and 'pot' was something you cooked in. 'Rock music' was a grandmother's lullaby, 'Eldorado' was an ice cream, and a 'gay' person was the life and soul of the party and nothing more, while 'aids' just meant beauty treatment or help for someone in trouble.

We who were born before 1940, must be a hardy bunch when you think of the way in which the world has changed and the adjustments we have had to make.

No wonder we are so confused and there is a generation gap today …

BUT …

By the grace of GOD … we have survived!

ALLELUIA!

THE WORLDS SHORTEST AND GREATEST FAIRY TALE

Once upon a time, a guy asked a girl, "Will you marry me?"

The girl said "NO!"

And the guy lived happily ever after and went fishing, hunting and played golf a lot and drank beer and farted whenever he wanted.

THE END

A FINAL THOUGHT ...

In writing and typing a book one gets tired ...

Yes, I'm tired. For several years I've been blaming it on middle age, poor blood, lack of vitamins, air pollution, saccharin, obesity, dieting, under arm odour, yellow wax build-up and another dozen maladies that make you wonder if life is really worth living.

But ... I found out it ain't that! I'm tired because I am overworked. The population of this country is 51 million; 21 million are retired. That leaves 30 million to do the work.

There are 19 million at school. That leaves 11 million to do the work.

Two million are unemployed and four million are employed by Government. That leaves five million to do the work.

One million are in the armed forces, which leave four million to do the work. Three million are employed by County and Borough Councils, leaving one million to do the work. There are 620,000 people in hospital and 379,998 in prisons, which leaves 2 people to do the work – you and me.

And you're sitting on your bum reading this ...

NO WONDER I'M TIRED!

If you have any similar funnies, I would be interested in writing/publishing Volume 2.

Please send any information to me for editing.

We could have a 1A volume:

THE PICTURE BOOK OF AMPHIGOURI ... and it's rude!

The contents of this book were taken during the time the author was in Post Office employment – his next book *Diary of a PRD Guru* pictures his exciting and lively roll in media and public relations – a picture book of events and stunts that will be published later this year.

CONSEQUENCES & CONCLUSIONS

Well we've poked fun at the civil service and government departments – are there consequences over the years of what the civil service and government of the day have done for us?

I well remember playing consequences at Christmas – everyone writes on a piece of paper and folds it over before someone else writes – it goes

A Boy   - meets   A Girl

At -some place

He said to her……..   She said to him……..

Then what they did……The consequence was…..

And the world said……

Anyway, it goes something like that and when you personalise it to people in the room or family or friends everyone knows it can be such fun.

However the story I finish with is all about Black Puddings -

I met a man in the post office who had worked in the civil service in London – Whitehall! He said as a junior clerk in the 1950s he was responsible for the weekly black pudding return listing the number of black puddings consumed each week in the north of England. He did this duty for a number of months before becoming suspicious about its purpose so he followed from his out-tray the black pudding return on its journey through the internal postal service.

The return ended up in a basement rooms with dusty old files and on examination there were black pudding returns going back many many years – back until 1898 – and at the back of the file was the reason. In the House of Commons an MP exclaimed during Prime Minsters questions – "It would be interesting to note how many black puddings are being eaten in northern England!"

So, on this 'over the shoulder comment' from an MP the civil service acted with enthusiasm and set up the complicated return process of listing the numbers of black puddings being eaten each week.

Wonder how much it cost – and indeed what is worth while recording for posterity. What have been the consequences and conclusions of the civic service and government on life as we know it? I hope this book has given you some thoughts about life!! Thank you for reading it.

Paul Diggens

www.ingramcontent.com/pod-product-compliance
Lightning Source LLC
Chambersburg PA
CBHW020612270326
41927CB00005B/304